AVERY YOUNG

Financial Literacy Explained: A Simple Guide for Those Who NEVER Got It

Practical Steps to Secure Your Financial Future: Mastering Savings, Investing, and Debt Management - No Prior Knowledge Required

Contents

Chapter 1

Introduction

"Being rich is having money; being wealthy is having time." - *Margaret Bonanno*

In today's world, financial freedom seems like an elusive goal for many, especially those who grew up without much guidance or access to financial resources. If you were raised in a household where money was never openly discussed, or perhaps where financial stress was a constant concern, it's easy to feel like you're stuck in a cycle of living paycheck to paycheck. But the truth is, financial freedom is possible for anyone, no matter where they start.

Starting from Scratch: How to Build a Strong Financial Foundation and Transform Your Future

Financial freedom isn't just about making more money—it's about learning how to manage the money you have, breaking free from the fears and limiting beliefs that have held you back, and creating a financial future that is secure, stress-free, and full of opportunities. It's about gaining control over your finances so that you can live the life you want, without worrying about where the next paycheck will come from or how you'll pay for unexpected expenses.

This book is for those who've never been taught the basics of money management—those who are ready to take control of their financial destiny, regardless of their starting point. Whether you've struggled with debt, lack of savings, or simply never had the tools to make smarter financial decisions, this is the resource that will help you turn things around.

Throughout this book, you will learn how to take practical steps toward financial literacy. From budgeting and saving, to understanding credit, building wealth, and even investing, these concepts will help you build a strong financial foundation. But this journey isn't just about numbers and strategies—it's about shifting your mindset. Financial literacy is as much about how you think about money as it is about how you manage it. Your mindset will shape your ability to make the right decisions, overcome challenges, and ultimately create the life you want.

You may have felt overwhelmed by money at times, thinking that financial freedom is only for the wealthy or those with special knowledge. But by learning the basic principles of financial literacy and applying them consistently, you'll begin to see change. No matter how small the steps, each decision you make towards financial stability builds momentum, bringing you closer to your goals.

In the following chapters, you'll gain the knowledge and confidence to:

- Take control of your spending and create a realistic budget that works for your lifestyle.
- Learn how to save for the future, protect yourself from emergencies, and build a financial cushion.
- Understand the importance of credit and how to improve your credit score.
- Discover the power of investing and how to grow your wealth, even with modest starting capital.
- Explore multiple income streams that can increase your financial security and help you reach your goals faster.

Most importantly, you will realize that you can take charge of your financial future, no matter your past or current situation. This book isn't just about information—it's about empowerment. It's about helping you feel confident in your ability to manage money, build wealth, and create lasting financial freedom for yourself and your family.

As you read, you'll find that small, consistent changes can lead to major improvements in your financial life. And with each step you take, you'll be setting yourself up for long-term success.

The journey to financial freedom starts with a single step—and you've already taken that step by picking up this book. Together, we'll break down the barriers to financial success and show you exactly how to create the future you've always wanted.

Are you ready to take control of your finances and build the life you deserve? Let's get started.

What is Financial Literacy?

At its core, **financial literacy** means having the knowledge and skills to manage your money effectively. It involves understanding how money works—how to earn it, save it, spend it, and invest it—so that you can make informed decisions and avoid common financial pitfalls. Financial literacy is more than just knowing what a budget is or how to use a credit card—it's about understanding the broader concepts of personal finance, including how to build wealth, plan for the future, and protect yourself financially.

For many, financial literacy is not something that was taught at home or in school. In fact, many people—especially those from lower-income backgrounds—often grow up with little to no formal financial education. As a result, they may struggle with making wise financial choices, saving money, or planning for their future. That's where this book comes in. The goal is to empower you with the knowledge and tools you need to take control of your financial life and make decisions that will improve your financial security.

Why Financial Literacy Matters

Financial literacy is critical because it directly impacts your ability to navigate the world of personal finance and achieve financial freedom. Without it, you might make financial decisions based on guesswork, bad advice, or limited knowledge, which can lead to stress, debt, and missed opportunities. Financial literacy helps you avoid these pitfalls and provides you with the tools you need to:

1. **Make Informed Decisions**: With financial literacy, you understand your options and can make smarter decisions about how to use your money. Whether you're buying a car, taking out a loan, or deciding how to save for retirement, being financially literate means you can weigh the pros and cons and choose the option that best suits your needs.

2. **Avoid Debt Traps**: Many people fall into the trap of debt because they don't understand how credit works or how to manage borrowing responsibly. Financial literacy teaches you how to use credit wisely, how to avoid high-interest loans, and how to get out of debt faster. It empowers you to make better choices about when to borrow, how to pay off debt, and how to avoid common debt traps like payday loans or credit card overuse.

3. **Build Wealth**: Financial literacy helps you understand the importance of saving and investing for the future. It teaches you how to create a budget, save for emergencies, and take advantage of opportunities like employer-sponsored retirement plans and investing in stocks or real estate. By being financially literate, you can learn to grow your wealth over time and work towards long-term financial goals.

4. **Protect Yourself from Financial Risks**: Life is unpredictable, and being financially literate can help you protect yourself from unexpected events like job loss, illness, or financial emergencies. Financial literacy teaches you the importance of insurance, building an emergency fund, and how to manage risk. It ensures that you have a safety net in place to weather life's uncertainties without jeopardizing your financial stability.

5. **Increase Financial Confidence**: When you understand how money works, you feel more in control of your financial situation. This confidence translates into better decision-making, less stress around money, and the ability to take charge of your financial future. Financial literacy helps you break free from the anxiety and uncertainty that often come with poor financial decisions, giving you the tools to move forward with confidence.

The Link Between Financial Knowledge and Financial Security

Financial literacy isn't just about understanding numbers and formulas—it's about empowerment. It allows you to take control of your finances and work toward building a life of financial security. The link between financial knowledge and financial security is undeniable. People who are financially literate tend to have:

- **Better control over their spending**: They understand the difference between needs and wants, which helps them make more conscious spending decisions and stick to a budget.
- **Stronger saving habits**: They recognize the importance of saving for the future and prioritize long-term goals like emergency funds, retirement savings, and homeownership.
- **A solid foundation for wealth-building**: Financially literate individuals are more likely to invest in assets like stocks, bonds, and real estate, which can generate passive income and build wealth over time.
- **Better protection against financial risks**: They understand how insurance works, the importance of credit, and how to safeguard themselves from financial crises, whether due to job loss, medical emergencies, or other unforeseen circumstances.

Financial literacy is an essential building block for creating financial freedom—the ability to live comfortably, without the constant worry of money, and with the flexibility to make choices based on your values and goals, rather than out of financial necessity.

Common Barriers to Financial Literacy

While the benefits of financial literacy are clear, many people face barriers that make it difficult to gain financial knowledge. These barriers can include:

- **Lack of access to resources**: Growing up in a low-income household or in a community where financial education wasn't prioritized can limit your exposure to basic financial concepts. Without role models or access to financial guidance, it's easy to feel lost or overwhelmed when it comes to money.
- **Cultural biases and money-blocking beliefs**: Many people carry **money-blocking beliefs** passed down from their families or cultures. These beliefs might include negative attitudes about wealth, the fear of talking about money, or the belief that financial success is only for certain people. These mental blocks can prevent individuals from seeking financial education or feeling confident in their ability to manage money effectively.
- **Fear and anxiety around money**: Financial stress is common, and it can be paralyzing. Fear of making the wrong financial decision, fear of debt, or a lack of confidence in managing money can prevent people from taking action to improve their financial situation. However, financial literacy helps to break down these fears by providing knowledge and practical tools to navigate the financial world with confidence.

How This Book Can Help

In this book, we'll guide you through the process of improving your financial literacy step by step. The goal is to take complex financial concepts and break them down into manageable, easy-to-understand pieces. By the end of this journey, you will have the tools and knowledge to:

- **Create and stick to a budget**
- **Build an emergency fund**
- **Understand how to use credit responsibly**
- **Start saving and investing for the future**
- **Overcome financial blocks and develop a positive money mindset**

This book is not about becoming rich overnight. It's about creating a solid financial foundation—one that enables you to manage your money, reduce financial stress, and start building the life you deserve. Whether you're starting from scratch or just looking to refine your financial strategies, this guide will empower you to take control of your financial future, step by step.

Financial Literacy as the Key to Unlocking Your Potential

Financial literacy is the key to unlocking your financial potential and achieving long-term security. Understanding the basics of money management, saving, investing, and overcoming mental barriers will not only help you achieve financial freedom but also give you the confidence to make smart, informed decisions for your future.

By the end of this book, you will no longer feel overwhelmed by financial decisions. Instead, you'll have the knowledge and skills to make smart choices, overcome obstacles, and create a financially secure and empowered life. Financial literacy is a journey, and the first step is to start learning and taking action today.

Chapter 2

Rewriting Your Financial Story: Building a Mindset for Success

"We can't become what we need to be by remaining what we are." - Oprah Winfrey

Your mindset about money plays a crucial role in your financial success. A limiting or money-blocking mindset can prevent you from achieving your financial goals. By recognizing and shifting these negative beliefs, you can develop a healthier relationship with money and set yourself up for a more secure financial future. In this chapter, we'll dive into what a money-blocking mindset looks like, explore common money-related thoughts that hold you back, and discuss practical ways to overcome them in a simple and actionable way.

What is a Money-Blocking Mindset?

A **money-blocking mindset** is when negative beliefs and attitudes about money prevent you from managing it effectively and achieving your financial goals. These thoughts can stem from messages you've absorbed from family, friends, or even media like TV shows and movies. With a money-blocking mindset, you might struggle to save, invest, or feel confident about your financial future.

Common Money-Blocking Beliefs

One common belief is thinking, "I don't deserve to have a lot of money." This might stem from the idea that only certain people are entitled to wealth. However, the reality is that everyone has the right to financial security and the opportunity to succeed.

Another limiting belief is that "money is bad." You may have heard that money is the root of all evil. While it's true that money can be misused, it can also be a powerful tool for good—whether it's helping others, supporting your family, or improving your own life.

You might also tell yourself, "I'll never be good with money," especially if you've made mistakes in the past. This kind of thinking can hold you back from learning and improving your financial habits.

Lastly, some people believe, "I need to spend money to be happy." This mindset can lead to overspending and debt. While buying things may bring temporary joy, true happiness comes from financial security and the ability to reach your goals.

Many first-generation Americans learn money-blocking mindsets from their immigrant families, often shaped by the struggles and financial limitations their families faced when they first arrived in the U.S. For example, parents might constantly emphasize the scarcity of money, saying things like, "We have to be careful with every dollar," or "Money is hard to come by." These messages often stem from the reality of having to work multiple jobs to make ends meet or the fear of not having enough. As a result, children may internalize the belief that money is something to be feared, or that having a lot of it makes people selfish or greedy.

Additionally, some immigrant families might place more value on hard work than on financial planning or investing. Phrases like, "Just work hard and everything will be fine," can lead children to believe that financial security comes solely from labor, rather than through strategic money management. This mindset can prevent them from exploring other paths to wealth, like saving, investing, or entrepreneurship, as they may not see these options as realistic or accessible. Consequently, the child may grow up with a limited view of money and struggle to break free from these ingrained beliefs, even if they find themselves in a position to build wealth.

How to Overcome a Money-Blocking Mindset

Changing the way you think about money begins with recognizing and challenging any negative beliefs you hold. Start by noticing when you have negative thoughts about money. Ask yourself where these beliefs come from and whether they're truly based in reality.

Learning more about money can boost your confidence. The more you understand about saving, investing, and managing your finances, the more equipped you'll feel to handle them. Consider reading books, taking online courses, or speaking with a financial advisor to expand your knowledge.

Setting realistic financial goals is also essential. Think about what you want to achieve and break it down into manageable steps. Celebrate your progress along the way to help you feel like you're making strides and stay motivated.

Surrounding yourself with people who have a healthy attitude toward money can make a big difference. Positive influences can offer support and encouragement, while it's wise to distance yourself from those who make you feel bad about your financial situation or push you toward reckless spending.

Practicing gratitude can shift your focus from what you don't have to what you do. Appreciating your current financial situation, no matter how small, can help foster a more positive outlook.

Finally, visualization is a powerful tool. Spend a few minutes each day imagining yourself achieving your financial goals. This simple practice can help keep you motivated and focused on the bigger picture.

Identify and Challenge Money-Beliefs

Many of us have developed money beliefs over the years, whether from our upbringing, cultural influences, or personal experiences. These beliefs shape how we view and interact with money. For example, if you were raised in a household where money was always a source of stress or scarcity, you might have internalized the belief that money is difficult to obtain or that it's hard to hold onto. On the other hand, if you grew up hearing "money doesn't grow on trees," you may carry a deep-seated belief that wealth is unattainable. The first step in changing your financial future is to recognize and challenge these limiting beliefs.

Write Down Your Beliefs About Money

Start by taking a moment to reflect on your thoughts and feelings about money. Write them down. Here are some examples to get you started:

- "Money is hard to come by."
- "I'll never be able to afford the things I want."
- "People with money are lucky or born into it."
- "I'm just not good with money."

Where Do These Beliefs Come From?

Once you've written down your beliefs, ask yourself where they came from. Did they come from your parents, teachers, or friends? Were they shaped by your financial struggles or experiences? Understanding where your money beliefs originate is important because it allows you to see that they are not set in stone—they are simply ideas that have been passed down or created based on past experiences.

Challenge Your Money Beliefs

Next, challenge these beliefs. Ask yourself if they are truly accurate or if they are just a reflection of your past experiences. For example, if you believe "money doesn't grow on trees," try reframing it to "money can be earned through hard work, smart decisions, and being resourceful." Here's how to challenge your beliefs:

1. **Question the belief**: Is this belief true? Where's the evidence?
2. **Reframe the belief**: What is a more empowering, realistic belief? *Instead of, "I'll never be rich," try, "I can build wealth over time with smart decisions."*
3. **Replace it**: Every time that limiting belief surfaces, replace it with a positive affirmation or new belief. *For instance, replace "I'll never afford a house" with "I am taking steps to improve my finances, and homeownership is within reach."*

Why Challenging These Beliefs Matters

Changing your money mindset is about more than just positive thinking—it's about giving yourself the power to take control of your financial future. By challenging limiting beliefs, you make space for new, empowering thoughts and actions that can lead to financial growth. The more you practice identifying and replacing negative beliefs, the more naturally these positive thoughts will become a part of your financial journey.

Transforming Your Mindset

Keep a journal of your money-related thoughts over the next week. Each time you catch yourself thinking a negative or limiting thought about money, write it down. Then, challenge that thought and reframe it with a more empowering belief. By the end of the week, you will begin to notice patterns in your thinking, and you'll be taking the first steps toward changing your money mindset.

Replace Negative Beliefs with Positive Affirmations

One of the most powerful tools in changing your money mindset is the practice of affirmations. Affirmations are positive, empowering statements that help you shift your thinking and reprogram your brain. When you replace your negative, money-blocking beliefs with positive affirmations, you begin to break free from financial self-doubt and start cultivating a mindset that attracts success.

Create Your Own Positive Money Affirmations

Start by developing a list of positive affirmations that challenge your limiting beliefs. These affirmations should be simple, empowering, and specific to your financial goals. The key is to make them believable and achievable. Here are a few examples:

- "I am capable of managing my money and building wealth."
- "I attract financial opportunities every day."
- "I am worthy of financial success and abundance."
- "I can make smart, informed decisions with my money."
- "Money flows easily into my life as I manage it responsibly."

Write down 3 to 5 affirmations that resonate with you. Feel free to adjust them so they feel authentic to your situation and goals.

Practice Affirmations Daily

The next step is to make affirmations a regular part of your routine. Set aside a few minutes each day, preferably in the morning, to recite your affirmations. You can say them out loud, write them down, or even repeat them silently in your head. The key is consistency and conviction. Here's how you can do it:

- **Morning Ritual**: As you wake up, before your day begins, stand in front of the mirror and repeat your affirmations. Visualize what it would feel like to live out these affirmations—imagine yourself making wise financial decisions, building savings, and feeling financially empowered.
- **During Difficult Moments**: Whenever you feel anxiety about money, such as when reviewing bills or making a purchase, pause and repeat your affirmations. It will help to calm your nerves and remind you of

your ability to take control of your finances.

- **Before Bed**: Reflect on your day and repeat your affirmations as you prepare to sleep. This will help reinforce the positive mindset while your brain is in a relaxed, receptive state.

Why Positive Affirmations Work

Affirmations work because they train your brain to focus on the possibilities rather than the limitations. When you repeat empowering statements, you create new neural pathways that align with success, confidence, and abundance. Over time, your beliefs will shift, and you'll start to feel more confident in your ability to handle money.

Studies have shown that positive affirmations can help improve self-esteem, reduce stress, and foster a more resilient mindset. By consistently repeating your affirmations, you actively change the way you view yourself and your financial future.

Mindset Transformation with the Power of Positive Affirmations

Each morning for the next week, choose a quiet moment to stand in front of the mirror and repeat your affirmations out loud. Visualize yourself successfully managing your finances—whether it's paying off debt, saving money, or making wise investment decisions. As you do this, focus on how it feels to have financial control, security, and success. Write down how this practice makes you feel after each session—are you less stressed, more confident, or more motivated?

In addition to morning practice, whenever negative thoughts about money arise, immediately replace them with your affirmations. For example, if you think, "I'll never get out of debt," stop and say, "I am on the path to becoming debt-free, and every small step is progress."

Track Your Progress

As you incorporate affirmations into your daily routine, keep a journal of any changes you notice in your thoughts and behaviors. Are you feeling more confident about making financial decisions? Are you more likely to stick to your budget or save money? Tracking these small wins will help reinforce the belief that your new mindset is already helping you take control of your financial future.

Set Small, Achievable Financial Goals

One of the most effective ways to shift your money mindset is by setting and achieving small, realistic financial goals. When you focus on small, actionable steps rather than the overwhelming picture of financial success, you can gradually build momentum, confidence, and a sense of control over your finances. Achieving these goals reinforces the belief that you are capable of improving your financial situation and making better decisions.

Break Down Your Goals into Manageable Steps

Start by identifying a financial goal you'd like to achieve. It could be something as simple as building an emergency fund, paying off a small debt, or saving for a specific purchase. The key is to make your goal specific, measurable, and realistic. Here's how you can break it down:

- **Specific**: Be clear about what you want to achieve. Instead of saying, "I want to save money," say, "I want to save $200 for an emergency fund."
- **Measurable**: Ensure the goal can be tracked. How will you know when you've reached it? For example, you can track your progress by adding up how much you save each week.
- **Achievable**: Make sure the goal is realistic. If saving $200 feels like too much, break it down into smaller weekly or monthly amounts. Start with saving $50 this month, then gradually increase it.

- **Time-bound**: Set a deadline to keep yourself on track. For example, "I will save $200 in the next two months."

Start with Small Wins

It's easy to get discouraged by big financial goals that seem impossible. Instead, focus on smaller, incremental achievements that will help you feel a sense of accomplishment. These small wins will keep you motivated and prove to you that you can make progress. Here are some examples of small financial goals:

- Save $50 in the next month for an emergency fund.
- Pay off a $100 credit card balance by the end of the next pay cycle.
- Cut unnecessary subscriptions and save $25 per month.
- Set aside 10% of your weekly income for savings or investment.

Each time you accomplish one of these smaller goals, you will not only feel empowered but will also begin to see how consistent, focused actions can lead to larger financial successes.

Why Small Goals Work

Starting small helps you avoid feeling overwhelmed. Many people are intimidated by their financial problems, but when they break their goals down into manageable steps, it becomes easier to take action. Small goals also allow you to see quick progress, which boosts motivation. It's important to remember that financial success isn't about a single large win, but rather a series of smaller, consistent steps that build on each other.

When you start achieving small goals, you'll begin to develop a sense of control over your money, and that confidence will spread to other areas of your financial life. Over time, these small steps will lead to big changes, such as building a strong savings habit, reducing debt, and even creating wealth.

Putting It Into Practice

Write down one or two small financial goals that you can realistically achieve within the next month. Make sure they are specific and measurable, like saving $50, cutting back on an unnecessary expense, or paying down a small debt. Track your progress daily or weekly and celebrate when you meet each goal. It's important to acknowledge and reward yourself for your successes, no matter how small.

For example, if your goal is to save $50, track every time you put money into your savings. When you hit the target, take a moment to recognize your achievement and reflect on how it feels to have made progress toward your financial goals.

Review and Adjust Your Goals Regularly

As you make progress with your goals, review them regularly. If you're meeting your targets comfortably, consider increasing the amount or setting a new goal. If you're finding it difficult, reassess the goal to make sure it's still realistic and achievable. The goal isn't to set yourself up for failure, but to create a path that feels challenging yet attainable.

Track and Celebrate Every Financial Win

Tracking your progress and celebrating small victories is an essential part of developing a positive money mindset. It's easy to focus on what you haven't achieved yet, but by recognizing and celebrating each win, you reinforce the belief that you are capable of making positive changes in your financial life. These small wins can build up over time, creating a sense of momentum and motivation to keep moving forward.

Keep a Financial Journal

Start by keeping a simple financial journal or tracker where you can record your financial wins, no matter how small. This could be a physical notebook, a digital document, or even an app that helps you track your progress. Every time you achieve something related to your financial goals, write it down. Some examples of wins to track include:

- Successfully sticking to your budget for the week.
- Saving a set amount of money (even if it's small).
- Paying off a portion of your debt.
- Negotiating a lower bill or saving on a purchase.
- Completing a financial task you've been putting off (like checking your credit score).

Tracking these wins helps you see how much progress you're making, even if it doesn't always feel like you're getting ahead. Over time, these small accomplishments will add up and create a sense of financial empowerment.

Celebrate Each Win

Once you've tracked a win, celebrate it. Celebrating doesn't have to mean spending money—it's about acknowledging your progress and rewarding yourself in a way that feels fulfilling. For example:

- Take a moment to reflect on how far you've come and how great it feels to accomplish a goal.
- Treat yourself to something meaningful (it could be a relaxing activity, a favorite snack, or a personal time-out to relax).
- Share your win with a supportive friend or family member who will celebrate with you and keep you motivated.

Celebrating your achievements reinforces the habit of financial success and reminds you that you are capable of reaching your goals. It also builds positive energy around your finances, making money management feel more rewarding.

Why Tracking and Celebrating Matter

Tracking and celebrating financial wins help to change your relationship with money. Instead of seeing finances as a source of stress, you begin to associate financial actions with positive emotions—motivation, accomplishment, and confidence. Each win, no matter how small, helps you break free from the feeling of being overwhelmed by money and puts you in control of your financial destiny.

By regularly tracking your progress and celebrating your wins, you reinforce the idea that financial success is a series of small, consistent actions that lead to big results. This creates momentum and motivates you to continue making smart financial decisions, no matter where you're starting from.

Educate Yourself: Learn Financial Terms and Concepts

One of the most empowering actions you can take to overcome a money-blocking mindset is to educate yourself about financial terms and concepts. Many people feel overwhelmed or anxious about money simply because they don't understand the terminology or the mechanics behind it. The more you know, the more control you'll feel over your financial decisions. Understanding the basics of personal finance—such as how budgeting works, how to save, and what investing is—will help you make informed decisions and take confident steps toward financial freedom.

Start with the Basics

Begin by learning some foundational financial terms that will empower you to take control of your money. Here are a few key concepts to start with:

- **Income**: The money you earn from your job, side hustle, or investments.
- **Expenses**: The money you spend on necessities (like rent, utilities, groceries) and non-essentials (like entertainment and dining out).
- **Savings**: The portion of your income you set aside for future use, typically in an emergency fund or savings account.
- **Debt**: Money you owe to others, such as credit card balances, loans, or mortgages.
- **Interest**: The cost of borrowing money or the earnings you get from saving or investing money.
- **Budget**: A plan that tracks how much money you have coming in and going out, helping you control your spending and saving.

Learn One New Term Every Week

Pick one new financial term each week to focus on and learn its meaning. Spend some time researching it, reading articles or watching videos online, or asking a knowledgeable friend or family member to explain it. Write down a brief definition of the term and note how it relates to your financial situation. Here's how to apply this:

- Week 1: Learn about credit scores—what they are, how they are calculated, and why they matter.
- Week 2: Learn about emergency funds—why it's essential to have one, how much to save, and where to put it.
- Week 3: Learn about interest rates—how they affect your debt and savings.

At the end of the week, take a few minutes to reflect on how understanding that term can help you make better financial decisions. For example, after learning about credit scores, you might realize that improving your score could help you save money on loans and credit cards.

Why Educating Yourself Matters

Knowledge is power. The more you understand about how money works, the less intimidated you'll feel about managing it. Financial literacy gives you the confidence to make smart choices, whether you're creating a budget, managing debt, or making investments. It helps you avoid costly mistakes, and over time, it can turn what once felt like a daunting task into something that is entirely manageable.

For example, once you understand how interest rates work, you can make smarter decisions about whether to pay off debt aggressively or take advantage of low-interest loans or credit cards. Understanding compound interest can show you the power of investing early, even with small amounts of money.

How to Take Action

Start by looking at your current financial situation and identify areas where you feel confused or uncertain. Do you know how your credit score is calculated? Are you unsure about the best way to save for retirement? Identify one area of confusion and make it a point to learn more about it.

Set aside time each week to learn a new concept related to your finances. Create a simple glossary for yourself, where you can add terms you've learned and jot down how they apply to your financial goals. The more you learn, the more capable and confident you'll become in handling your money.

Make Financial Education a Habit

Reading books, following blogs, or listening to podcasts about personal finance can also help you build a more robust financial vocabulary. Some helpful resources include:

- Blogs and websites like **NerdWallet** or **The Balance**, which provide easy-to-understand financial advice.

- Podcasts like **The Dave Ramsey Show** or **BiggerPockets** that focus on real-world personal finance and investing advice.
- YouTube channels like **The Financial Diet** or **Investopedia** for beginners looking to understand finance in simple terms.

Remember, the more you educate yourself, the more control you'll have over your financial future. It's an ongoing process, but each step you take builds your financial knowledge and confidence.

Surround Yourself with Positive Financial Role Models

The people we surround ourselves with can have a significant impact on our financial mindset and habits. Having positive financial role models—whether in real life or through books, podcasts, or social media—can inspire and motivate us to make better money decisions. These role models help shift our perspective on what's possible, teach us practical money management skills, and provide guidance on how to overcome financial challenges.

Find Financial Role Models in the Public Eye

Even if you don't have a personal mentor, you can still find inspiration from others who have mastered their finances. These role models might not be someone you know personally, but they can still teach you valuable lessons.

These public role models offer practical advice and inspiration that can help you overcome financial challenges. While they may not know you personally, their experiences and lessons can still guide you on your journey.

Learn from Their Success

Once you've identified a financial role model, start learning from their experiences. Read their books, listen to their podcasts, or watch their videos. Pay attention to the strategies they used to improve their finances and ask yourself: "How can I apply this to my life?" You don't need to follow everything they do, but their experiences can offer valuable lessons that you can adapt to your own circumstances.

Why Financial Role Models Matter

The truth is, having a financial role model—whether they're a person you know or someone you follow online—can help you see that financial success is possible, even if you didn't grow up learning about money. They show you that it's possible to make smart choices, get out of debt, and build wealth, regardless of your starting point. Financial role models inspire and remind you that you can take control of your finances, too.

Even if you've never had someone in your life to teach you about managing money, learning from others' experiences can give you the knowledge and confidence to make better financial decisions. Role models also help you see that small changes in behavior can lead to big results over time. When you see others achieving financial success, it shows you that it's not only possible but that you can do it, too.

Putting It Into Practice

Take a few minutes today to research at least one financial role model whose journey resonates with you. This could be someone who started with little but built wealth through smart money habits. Watch one of their videos, read an article, or pick up a book they've written. As you learn, jot down key lessons that stand out to you. Afterward, think about how you can apply one of those lessons to your own financial situation.

If you can't find a specific person to follow right now, start by joining online communities or forums where people share their financial journeys and advice. Websites like Reddit or Facebook groups dedicated to budgeting and saving are great places to connect with others who are focused on improving their finances.

Build Your Own Financial Support Network

In addition to role models, consider building a network of supportive people who are on a similar financial journey. This could be an online group, a budgeting partner, or even a friend or family member you trust to talk about money with. Surrounding yourself with people who share similar goals can help keep you motivated and accountable.

When you don't have someone personally guiding you, learning from others—whether virtually or in books—can help you feel like you're not alone on this journey.

Practice Gratitude and Shift Focus from Scarcity to Abundance

One of the most powerful mindset shifts you can make is to change the way you think about money from a place of scarcity to a place of abundance. Many people grow up with the belief that there is never enough money or that financial opportunities are limited. This mindset of scarcity can block your ability to build wealth, save, and take the actions necessary to improve your financial situation. Practicing gratitude and focusing on abundance helps break this cycle by fostering a mindset of opportunity, growth, and possibility.

Start a Gratitude Journal

A simple but powerful way to shift your mindset is by practicing daily gratitude. Gratitude helps you focus on what you already have, instead of what you lack, and it can transform how you view money and your financial situation. By acknowledging and appreciating the small things, you train your brain to see opportunities instead of obstacles. Here's how to get started:

- **Set aside a few minutes each day**: Choose a time each day, preferably in the morning or before bed, to reflect on what you're grateful for.
- **Write down 3 things**: Every day, write down three things you're thankful

for—these can be anything from the small (e.g., "I'm thankful for my morning coffee") to the big (e.g., "I'm grateful for the job that helps me provide for my family").

- **Include financial gratitude**: Try to include something related to your finances each day. For example: "I'm thankful for the opportunity to save $10 this week" or "I'm grateful for the financial lessons I'm learning."

By making gratitude a habit, you shift your focus from what's lacking to what's abundant in your life. This shift in perspective helps you approach financial challenges with a sense of optimism, reducing stress and building confidence in your ability to improve your financial situation.

Reframe Negative Thoughts About Money

When you catch yourself thinking negatively about money—such as "I'll never get out of debt" or "I'll never afford a house"—pause and reframe those thoughts into positive ones that align with abundance:

- Instead of, "I'm never going to be able to pay off my debt," try, "I'm making progress with every payment, and I'll be debt-free one step at a time."
- Instead of, "There's no way I'll ever be able to save enough for retirement," try, "Every dollar I save today brings me closer to financial freedom in the future."
- Instead of, "Money is always tight," try, "I am learning to manage my money in a way that helps me feel secure and in control."

By catching and reframing negative thoughts, you start to focus on growth, progress, and solutions rather than obstacles. This shift toward an abundance mindset opens the door to greater financial success.

Why an Abundance Mindset Matters

When you adopt an abundance mindset, you begin to see the world of money as full of opportunities, rather than limitations. This mindset encourages you to take positive actions, like budgeting, saving, and investing, because you believe there is always room for growth and improvement. Instead of feeling defeated by financial challenges, you start to look for ways to solve problems and find new opportunities.

An abundance mindset also helps you let go of feelings of guilt, shame, or envy when it comes to money. It allows you to appreciate what you have while striving for more, without the toxic stress of constantly comparing yourself to others or feeling like you're "behind."

Moving Forward

For the next week, make gratitude a part of your daily routine:

1. Each day, write down at least three things you're grateful for—include something related to your finances.
2. When negative thoughts about money arise, immediately reframe them into positive, abundance-focused thoughts.
3. At the end of the week, reflect on how this practice made you feel. Did it change how you approached your finances? Were you able to notice more opportunities for growth?

After a week, review the progress you've made with your mindset. Have you started feeling more optimistic about your financial future? Are you noticing more opportunities to improve your situation, even if they seem small? Continue to make gratitude a daily habit, and see how it shifts your entire approach to money.

Visualize Financial Success

Visualization is a powerful tool for achieving your financial goals because it helps you see your success before it happens. When you can vividly imagine yourself achieving your financial goals, it helps create a clear path for how to get there, boosts motivation, and strengthens your belief that it's possible. Visualization connects your thoughts and emotions to your goals, making them feel more achievable and real. The more you can see yourself succeeding, the more likely you are to take the actions needed to make that vision a reality.

Create a Vision for Your Financial Future

Take a moment to think about what financial success looks like for you. This could include getting out of debt, saving for an emergency fund, purchasing a home, or building a comfortable retirement. Close your eyes and imagine yourself already achieving these goals. What does it feel like? How does it impact your life? What does your day-to-day routine look like now that you've reached your financial goals?

Here's how you can visualize your financial success:

- **Picture the end result**: Imagine yourself debt-free or with a fully funded emergency savings account. Picture the emotions you would feel—relief, confidence, and pride. What does that success look like to you?
- **See the steps involved**: Visualize the small steps it will take to get there. Maybe you picture yourself sticking to a budget, making a savings deposit, or paying off a credit card.
- **Engage your senses**: The more detailed and real your visualization, the more powerful it will be. Imagine the sights, sounds, and emotions that come with achieving your goals. How does it feel to finally be in control of your finances?

Create a Vision Board

To make your vision more tangible, create a vision board—a physical or digital collage that visually represents your financial goals. A vision board helps turn abstract desires into clear, actionable goals:

- **Collect images, words, and quotes**: Find pictures that represent your financial dreams, whether it's a house you'd like to own, a vacation you'd love to take, or an image that symbolizes financial security.
- **Arrange them on a board or digital platform**: Use a corkboard, poster board, or even a digital platform like Pinterest to display your vision. Make sure it's something you can see often, like in your bedroom or office, so that you're constantly reminded of your goals.
- **Add motivating words or affirmations**: Include phrases like "Financial freedom is possible," "Every day, I am getting closer to my goals," or "I can achieve financial independence."

Seeing these images and reminders every day helps keep you focused and motivated, reinforcing the belief that your financial dreams are achievable.

Why Visualization Works

Visualization works because it taps into the power of the mind. By picturing your success, you train your brain to believe it's possible. This strengthens your motivation and focus, making it easier to take the necessary actions to make your goals a reality. Studies have shown that athletes and successful people in all fields use visualization techniques to prepare for success, and it can work just as powerfully in personal finance.

When you can see yourself succeeding financially, it helps to bridge the gap between where you are now and where you want to be. Your brain starts to think of ways to make it happen, helping you stay motivated and take the steps necessary to reach your goals.

For the next week, dedicate at least 5 minutes every day to visualization. Follow these steps:

1. **Find a quiet space**: Sit in a comfortable spot where you can relax and focus.
2. **Close your eyes and imagine your financial success**: Picture yourself achieving a specific financial goal, such as paying off a debt or saving for a house. See the details clearly, including how it feels, what it looks like, and the steps you took to get there.
3. **Engage with your vision board**: If you've created one, spend a few minutes each day looking at your vision board. Imagine yourself living the life represented in the images. Feel the emotions of success.

At the end of the week, reflect on how you feel. Did this practice help you stay focused on your goals? Do you feel more motivated to take actions toward achieving your financial success?

Practice Mindful Spending

Improving your financial mindset and habits can be challenging, especially if you've never had someone to guide you in the right direction. Seeking support from a financial mentor or group can provide you with the guidance, encouragement, and accountability you need to stay on track. Whether you find a mentor who has experience with managing money, or join a group of like-minded individuals, surrounding yourself with people who are focused on financial growth can significantly enhance your progress and keep you motivated on your journey.

Find a Financial Mentor

A financial mentor is someone who has experience with money management and is willing to share their knowledge and wisdom with you. A mentor doesn't have to be a financial expert, but they should have practical experience in managing money, saving, budgeting, or investing. Here's how to find a mentor:

- **Look within your network**: Start by asking family members, friends, or colleagues who have successfully managed their finances. Many people would be happy to offer advice or support, especially if you express a genuine desire to improve your financial situation.
- **Seek out professionals**: If you don't have someone in your immediate circle, consider hiring a financial advisor or coach. They can provide personalized guidance based on your unique financial situation, helping you set and achieve your goals.
- **Reach out to community organizations**: Many local nonprofits and community centers offer free financial literacy programs or mentorship opportunities. These organizations may have volunteers or experts who are willing to guide you on your financial journey.

A mentor can help you identify areas for improvement, offer advice on how to overcome financial challenges, and provide accountability as you work toward your goals.

Join a Financial Support Group

If you can't find a one-on-one mentor, consider joining a financial support group. These groups consist of people who are working on similar financial goals, and they offer a sense of community, encouragement, and shared resources. If you don't want to join a large group, consider finding an accountability partner—someone who you can check in with regularly about your progress, challenges, and successes. This could be a friend, family member, or colleague who is also working on their finances.

Support groups offer a sense of camaraderie, knowing you're not alone in your journey. The group can provide encouragement, share tips, and keep you motivated during times when you might feel discouraged.

Why Support Matters

Having a mentor or support group increases your chances of success because it provides several key benefits:

Regular check-ins with a mentor or support group can help keep you motivated and on track by holding you accountable for your progress, encouraging you to stay committed to your goals. Mentors and groups often provide expert advice and practical tips for overcoming financial challenges, whether you're struggling to stick to a budget or need guidance on investing. Additionally, when faced with setbacks, a mentor or group can offer encouragement, reminding you that financial growth is a journey with both successes and challenges.

At the end of the week, reflect on how having support helped you feel more confident and motivated about your financial journey. Did it provide you with new insights, encouragement, or practical advice that you can apply to your goals?

Leverage Online Communities and Resources

If you're unable to find a mentor or local group, you can still find valuable support and guidance through online resources. There are countless free or low-cost communities and platforms where you can learn, share, and interact with others who are on similar financial journeys. Here's how to tap into those resources:

Online forums and communities, such as those on Reddit, provide a platform where people can share financial experiences, ask questions, and offer advice, allowing you to learn from others and share your progress. Social media and blogs are also valuable resources, with financial influencers on platforms like Instagram, YouTube, and Twitter offering tips, advice, and inspiration to help improve financial literacy and wealth-building. Additionally, free online courses and webinars from websites like Coursera, Khan Academy, and YouTube provide self-paced learning opportunities on essential financial topics such as budgeting, saving, and investing, complementing your financial education.

Be Your Own Accountability Partner

Sometimes, the best way to stay motivated is to become your own accountability partner. By holding yourself responsible for your progress, you can develop the discipline and consistency needed to reach your financial goals. Here's how to do it:

- **Set weekly check-ins**: At the end of each week, sit down and review your progress. Ask yourself:
- Did I stick to my budget this week?
- What financial goals did I make progress on?
- Where did I struggle, and what can I do to improve next week?
- **Journal your journey**: Keep a financial journal where you can reflect on your challenges, successes, and lessons learned. Writing down your thoughts can help you stay focused and organized while also providing clarity about your financial priorities.
- **Use apps to track your goals**: Many financial apps allow you to set goals and track your progress. Some apps even have built-in reminders and reports that can help you stay accountable. Popular apps like Mint, YNAB (You Need a Budget), or even simple goal-tracking apps like Habitica can provide the structure and reminders you need to stay on course.

Why Self-Support Matters

While having external support is valuable, learning to be self-sufficient and resourceful is equally important. By creating your own accountability system and tapping into online resources, you build the confidence and discipline necessary to take control of your financial future. The key to success is consistency—by taking small, intentional actions each day, you can make significant progress toward your goals, even without a mentor or group.

Remember, financial growth is a journey, and everyone moves at their own pace. Whether you find support in the form of a mentor, group, or self-directed strategies, what matters most is staying committed and taking consistent action. With the right mindset and tools, you can achieve the financial freedom you desire.

Chapter 3

Mastering Spending and Creating a Financial Plan That Works

"Too many people spend money they earned..to buy things they don't want..to impress people that they don't like." — Will Rogers

Before you can save and grow your money, you first need to understand how to manage what you spend. Spending wisely is not just about cutting out all the things you enjoy; it's about being conscious of where your money goes and making sure you're prioritizing the things that truly matter to your financial well-being. The way you spend today has a direct impact on your ability to save and build a secure future.

Understanding Your Spending Habits

A good starting point is to look at how much you're spending and where that money is going. We often don't realize how small, daily purchases can add up over time. You might not realize that spending $10 a day on lunch or dinner can quickly add up to $3,650 over the course of a year.

Small purchases can quickly eat into your budget, leaving you with less money to save. But the good news is, once you identify these spending habits, you can start making small changes to redirect your money into savings.

The key to saving money is spending less than you earn. When you make conscious decisions about your spending, you'll naturally free up more money to put toward your savings goals. Even small amounts of savings can add up over time, and as your savings grow, it gives you more financial freedom and security.

Choosing to Set Limits on Small Essentials

Some people believe that setting limits on small essentials—like a daily coffee or lunch—might not be necessary because they're just small expenses. After all, it can feel like these things don't make a big impact on your finances. But the truth is, it's your choice how you manage your spending. There's no "one size fits all" when it comes to budgeting, and some may feel comfortable spending freely on small things. However, when you decide to limit those small expenses, it can free up money that can be invested in ways that truly benefit your future.

For example, let's say you choose to cut back on spending $5 a day on a snack or drink. That might seem small, but over a month, that's $150 you could save. Instead of spending that money on something temporary, you could use it to build an emergency fund or invest in your future.

By limiting spending on small, unnecessary things, you're not depriving yourself. You're choosing to redirect that money in ways that will have a more lasting and positive impact on your financial future. It's all about making small decisions today that will help you reach bigger goals down the road.

Living Paycheck to Paycheck: Breaking the Cycle

Living paycheck to paycheck is a reality for many people, especially when finances are tight or there isn't a clear plan in place for managing money. If you find yourself barely scraping by each month, with just enough to cover bills and expenses, it can feel overwhelming. The fear of not having enough money to cover an emergency or even basic needs is stressful, but it doesn't have to be permanent.

Why This Happens

Living paycheck to paycheck often happens when there's little to no room between income and expenses. There are several reasons this can occur:

- **High living costs**: Rent, utilities, food, and transportation costs might take up most of your paycheck, leaving little for savings.
- **Debt**: If you have outstanding loans or credit card debt, much of your paycheck goes toward paying interest and minimum payments, leaving less for other essentials.
- **Lack of financial planning**: Without a clear budget or plan, it's easy for money to slip through your fingers without you even realizing where it went.

Breaking the Cycle

The good news is that you can break free from living paycheck to paycheck by making small, intentional changes.

When it comes to improving your financial situation, you have two main options: managing your current income better through budgeting or increasing your income. Both are valid strategies, and which one you focus on may depend on your current circumstances. However, it's important to understand that either choice can help you move closer to financial stability and break free from the cycle of living paycheck to paycheck.

It's Worth It

Breaking the cycle of living paycheck to paycheck won't happen overnight, but every small step you take towards saving, budgeting, and reducing debt brings you closer to financial freedom. It's not about earning more money, but rather about making your money work for you. As you start managing your finances better, you'll begin to feel more in control, less stressed, and more confident in your ability to handle whatever comes your way.

Living paycheck to paycheck doesn't have to be your reality forever. With the right tools and mindset, you can take charge of your finances and build a more stable, secure future for yourself and your family. The first step is simple: decide that you want to change, and start small.

Taking Control of Your Finances

Budgeting is one of the most important tools you can use to take control of your finances. It's not just about restricting your spending or tracking every penny—it's about understanding where your money goes, making intentional decisions, and ensuring that you're using your income in a way that aligns with your goals. Whether you're trying to pay off debt, save for an emergency fund, or build wealth, a solid budget is the foundation that helps you get there.

Helps You Live Within Your Means

The primary purpose of a budget is to make sure you're not spending more than you earn. When you don't have a budget, it's easy to overspend, especially when you're not tracking every purchase. You may not realize how small, frequent purchases (like takeout, coffee, or shopping) add up over time. With a budget, you get a clear picture of your income and expenses, so you can avoid overspending and start living within your means.

Provides Clarity and Control

Budgeting gives you a sense of clarity and control over your financial situation. Instead of feeling stressed or anxious about where your money is going, you can make informed decisions about your spending. When you see exactly how much you have for necessities, savings, and discretionary spending, you're in control. This knowledge empowers you to take action, whether it's cutting back in certain areas or putting extra money toward your savings goals.

Saving for the Future

One of the biggest benefits of budgeting is that it allows you to save. When you don't have a budget, saving often feels impossible, especially when money is tight. However, by setting aside a portion of your income each month—no matter how small—you build the habit of saving. Over time, these small amounts add up, whether you're saving for an emergency fund, a big purchase, or your retirement. A budget helps you prioritize saving and ensures that you're always setting aside money for the future.

Makes Debt Repayment Easier

If you're carrying debt, budgeting is essential for paying it down. Without a budget, it's easy to let payments slip or pay only the minimum amount due, which keeps you stuck in a cycle of debt. A budget helps you allocate extra money each month toward paying off high-interest debt (like credit cards) or student loans. With a clear plan in place, you can focus on eliminating debt faster and paying it off more effectively.

Reduces Stress and Creates Financial Security

When you know exactly where your money is going, you're less likely to stress about financial surprises. A budget helps you plan for bills, emergencies, and even fun activities, so you're not caught off guard. It also allows you to prepare for future expenses, like car repairs or medical bills, which can be major sources of stress if you're not prepared. With a budget, you can start building a financial cushion and work toward greater financial security.

The First Step to Financial Confidence: Start Your Budget

A budget is the cornerstone of financial confidence because it gives you control over your money. When you have a clear understanding of where your money is going and how much you have available, you can make more informed, confident decisions about your spending, saving, and future financial goals.

A budget is essential for building financial confidence because it gives you clarity and control over your money. By tracking your income and expenses, you can make informed decisions, stay on track with your spending, and reduce the stress of financial uncertainty. A budget not only helps you manage your day-to-day expenses but also enables you to save for the future, pay down debt, and build wealth, creating a sense of security and empowering you to make proactive financial choices.

List Your Income

The first step in creating a budget is to clearly identify how much money you have coming in each month. This is important because it sets the foundation for all the other budgeting steps. Without knowing your income, you can't accurately plan your expenses or savings goals.

- **Include all sources of income**: Write down all the money you receive on a regular basis. This includes your salary, wages, any side hustles, or additional income streams (like freelance work, child support, or a rental property).
- **Use your net income**: Focus on the amount you take home after taxes and deductions, not your gross income. This is the money you can actually spend or save.

For example, if you earn $2,500 a month from your job and $500 from a side hustle, your total monthly income would be $3,000. Knowing your income is essential because it helps you set realistic limits for your spending and ensures that you're not budgeting for more than you actually have. It also allows you to see if there's any extra income you could use for savings or debt repayment. By starting with a clear picture of your income, you can confidently move forward with the next steps in budgeting.

Track Your Expenses

Once you've listed your income, the next step is to track your expenses. This is crucial because it helps you understand where your money is going and gives you the information you need to make adjustments. By knowing how much you're spending and on what, you can identify areas where you might be overspending and where you can cut back to make room for savings.

1. **List all your fixed expenses**: These are the regular, monthly payments that stay the same each month, such as rent, utilities, insurance, and loan payments.
2. **Track your variable expenses**: These are the things that change from month to month, like groceries, gas, entertainment, and dining out.
3. **Use an app or a simple spreadsheet**: You can use budgeting apps like Mint or YNAB, or even a notebook to jot down every expense. The key is consistency—write down everything you spend, no matter how small.
4. **Review your spending habits**: After tracking for a month, look at where your money is going. Are there areas where you could spend less or make adjustments? For example, could you cook at home more instead of eating out?

By tracking your expenses, you get a clear picture of your spending habits, and this will help you make smarter decisions about where to allocate your money, ultimately giving you more control over your finances.

Set Your Financial Goals

Now that you have a clear picture of your income and expenses, the next step is to set your financial goals. Whether you're saving for an emergency fund, paying off debt, or planning for a big purchase, setting specific and realistic goals will give you something to work towards and help you stay motivated.

1. **Define your goals**: Start by identifying what you want to achieve

financially. Be specific. For example, instead of just saying "save money," set a goal like "save $1,000 for an emergency fund" or "pay off $500 in credit card debt."

2. **Break them down**: Large goals can feel overwhelming, so break them down into smaller, manageable steps. For example, if your goal is to save $1,000 in six months, aim to save $167 per month.

3. **Set a timeline**: Decide when you want to achieve each goal. Giving yourself a timeframe helps keep you accountable and on track.

4. **Prioritize**: If you have multiple goals, determine which ones are most urgent. For example, paying off high-interest debt might take priority over saving for a vacation. Focus on one or two goals at a time to make progress without feeling overwhelmed.

By setting clear, achievable goals, you'll have a roadmap to follow, making it easier to stay focused and motivated to improve your financial situation.

Create a Budget and Allocate Your Money

After setting your financial goals, the next step is to create a budget that aligns with those goals. A budget is your financial plan—it helps you allocate your income towards your expenses, savings, and debt repayment in a way that supports your priorities. By sticking to your budget, you'll make sure that every dollar you earn is working toward your goals.

1. **Assign amounts to each category**: Based on your income and tracked expenses, decide how much money you'll allocate to each category.
2. **Essentials**: Rent, utilities, groceries, transportation.
3. **Savings**: Emergency fund, retirement, or other savings goals.
4. **Debt**: Pay off loans, credit cards, or other outstanding debts.
5. **Discretionary spending**: Entertainment, dining out, shopping, etc.
6. **Use the 75/15/10 rule (or a similar approach)**: A simple guideline is to allocate your income is 75% of your income to essentials and discretionary spending (wants and needs), 15% to savings and 10% to

investment. Or a similar approach that works best with your financial goals.

7. **Adjust as needed**: If you find that certain categories need more attention (like debt repayment or savings), consider cutting back on discretionary spending. If you're unsure where to cut, start with areas like dining out, subscriptions, or impulse buys.

8. **Track your progress**: Once you've set your budget, stick to it! Regularly check in on your expenses to make sure you're staying within your set limits. If you overspend in one category, adjust the next month.

By creating a budget and allocating your income thoughtfully, you ensure that your money is being spent in a way that brings you closer to your goals, rather than draining your funds without a plan. A solid budget is the foundation of financial success, helping you manage your day-to-day finances while prioritizing what's most important to you.

Review and Adjust Your Budget Regularly

The final step in the budgeting process is to regularly review and adjust your budget to ensure it's working for you. Life is unpredictable, and your expenses, income, or goals may change over time. By reviewing your budget regularly, you can make necessary adjustments, stay on track with your goals, and continue to build financial confidence.

1. **Track your actual spending**: At the end of each month, compare your actual spending to what you planned in your budget. Did you spend more on groceries? Did you save less than you intended? Tracking these differences helps you understand where you might need to make adjustments.

2. **Assess your progress toward goals**: Check in on your financial goals. Are you on track to meet your savings target? Have you paid down debt as planned? If you're behind, determine what changes you need to make to catch up.

3. **Identify areas to cut back**: If you're overspending in certain areas, figure out where you can trim back. Maybe you're spending too much on entertainment or eating out. Look for easy ways to adjust, like cooking at home more often or finding cheaper alternatives.

4. **Account for life changes**: Your income or expenses might change—whether it's a raise at work, an unexpected bill, or a new financial goal. Make sure your budget reflects these changes. For example, if you get a bonus, you might decide to put that extra money toward debt repayment or saving for a big purchase.

5. **Stay flexible**: A budget is a tool, not a rigid rule. If something isn't working, don't be afraid to change it. The key is to remain flexible while still keeping your long-term goals in mind.

By regularly reviewing and adjusting your budget, you ensure that your financial plan continues to support your needs and goals. This ongoing process keeps you in control of your money, and over time, it will help you feel more confident in your financial decisions and progress.

Chapter 4

Saving Made Simple: How to Build Your Financial Safety Net (Even When It's Not Fun)

"Success consists of going from failure to failure without loss of enthusiasm." -
Winston Churchill

When it comes to managing your finances, one of the most important decisions you'll face is how to improve your situation: should you focus on saving more, or should you try to increase your income? Both are essential strategies, and understanding how each one works can help you make informed choices.

Building Your Savings: The Key to Financial Security

For many people, saving money can feel like a daunting task, especially when it feels like there's never enough at the end of the month. But the truth is, saving is one of the most important steps you can take to improve your financial situation. Whether it's building an emergency fund, saving for a big purchase, or planning for retirement, setting aside money today can create more security and freedom in the future.

The good news is, saving doesn't have to be complicated or require a large income. By starting small and making consistent contributions, anyone can build savings that will help them feel more in control of their financial future.

Building a Savings Habit

Building a savings habit is one of the most empowering steps you can take toward financial stability. It's about creating a routine where setting aside money becomes automatic and prioritized, no matter how small the amount. When you make saving a habit, you create a safety net that allows you to feel more secure, ready for the unexpected, and closer to achieving your long-term financial goals.

Saving money provides a sense of security, especially in times of need. Life can be unpredictable, with unexpected expenses like car repairs or medical bills popping up without warning. Having a savings buffer, such as an emergency fund, ensures that you're not caught off guard by these costs. Instead of scrambling to find money or relying on credit cards or loans, you'll have the peace of mind knowing that you can manage the situation with the funds you've already set aside.

In addition, saving consistently allows you to prepare for future goals, whether it's buying a home, starting a business, or going on a vacation. Over time, your savings can grow, enabling you to fund these big purchases without falling into debt or depending on outside help. The more you save, the closer you get to achieving the things you want in life.

Perhaps one of the most significant benefits of saving is the reduction of financial stress. Without savings, unexpected expenses can feel overwhelming, and every financial challenge can feel like a crisis. But once you've built even a small cushion, you'll feel more in control and less anxious when things go wrong. Knowing that you have a financial safety net gives you the confidence to handle life's challenges calmly and without panic.

Different Types of Savings

There are several types of savings, each with its own purpose and benefits. Understanding the different types can help you choose the right one for your financial goals.

Emergency Savings

An emergency fund is one of the most crucial financial tools you can have. It's your safety net, designed to protect you from unexpected events that could otherwise disrupt your financial stability. Life is unpredictable, and things like car repairs, medical bills, or sudden job loss can happen at any time. Without an emergency fund, you might find yourself relying on credit cards or loans to cover these costs, leading to debt and potentially delaying your financial goals. Having an emergency fund ensures that you have the money on hand to deal with these surprises, allowing you to stay on track and avoid unnecessary stress.

Life can throw challenges your way, no matter how much you plan. Medical emergencies, like a sudden illness or injury, can lead to high bills that may not be fully covered by insurance. Similarly, if you lose your job or experience a decrease in income, an emergency fund can help you meet essential living expenses while you search for new opportunities. Unexpected car or home repairs, such as a broken-down vehicle or a leaking roof, can also drain your finances if you're unprepared. Even family emergencies, like needing to support a loved one who's fallen ill, can create urgent financial demands. An emergency fund provides the cushion you need to manage these situations without disrupting your financial goals or putting you into debt.

Short-Term Savings: Planning for the Near Future

Short-term savings are crucial for achieving financial goals that are within the next one to three years. Unlike long-term savings, which are often geared toward retirement or other distant goals, short-term savings focus on the things you want to accomplish sooner, like purchasing a car, going on vacation, or building an emergency fund. While it may seem less urgent than saving for long-term goals, having short-term savings is vital because it ensures that you're financially prepared for upcoming expenses without relying on credit cards or loans.

The beauty of short-term savings is that it gives you the flexibility to plan for and manage upcoming needs and desires without adding unnecessary financial stress. These goals are typically more immediate and tangible, and having the funds set aside for them can bring a sense of financial security and accomplishment. Instead of scrambling to find money at the last minute or relying on debt to cover these costs, short-term savings help you feel in control of your spending and allow you to achieve your goals without the added burden of high-interest debt.

For example, if you plan to buy a car in the next year, it's wise to start setting aside money specifically for that purchase. This allows you to avoid high-interest auto loans or even leasing, which can become an additional financial strain. Similarly, if you're looking forward to a vacation, saving for it ahead of time lets you enjoy the trip without the worry of paying for it later or charging it to a credit card.

One of the biggest benefits of short-term savings is that it allows you to remain flexible. Unlike long-term savings, which are typically tied up in investments or retirement accounts that are difficult to access, short-term savings are meant for the here and now. Having money set aside for near-term needs or desires can reduce financial stress, help you stay on track with your goals, and prevent you from relying on credit or loans for things that you can plan for in advance.

Where to Keep Your Short-Term Savings

Since short-term savings are designed to be accessible when you need them, they should be kept in accounts that offer both safety and liquidity. This means the money should be easy to access when you're ready to use it, but also protected from market fluctuations that could impact its value.

A **high-yield savings account** is an excellent choice for short-term savings because it offers better interest rates than regular savings accounts while still keeping your money safe. These accounts are also easy to access, making them ideal for savings that you plan to use within the next few years.

Another option is a **money market account**. These accounts often offer slightly higher interest rates than regular savings accounts but might come with certain requirements like a higher minimum balance or limited withdrawals. However, they are still low-risk and easily accessible when needed.

For those who prefer a more structured savings option, **Certificates of Deposit (CDs)** might be a good fit. While they typically offer higher interest rates than savings accounts, they lock your money in for a specific term. For short-term goals, a CD with a term that matches your savings goal—say, six months to a year—can help you earn a bit more while still providing the certainty that your money will be available when you need it.

Long-Term Savings: Securing Your Future

Long-term savings are the foundation for achieving financial goals that are years, or even decades, away. While short-term savings may cover immediate needs and desires, long-term savings are aimed at providing for your future financial security. This could include saving for retirement, buying a home, paying for your children's education, or building wealth to ensure a comfortable lifestyle as you age.

The key difference between short-term and long-term savings is the amount of time you have to save and invest. Because long-term savings are meant for distant goals, you have the advantage of time, which allows your money to grow and potentially work for you through compounding and investing.

Saving for long-term goals is important because it gives you the financial stability and peace of mind needed to live your life without constantly worrying about your financial future. For example, retirement may feel far off, but the earlier you start saving, the better prepared you'll be. The same goes for any other long-term financial goals—having a plan in place today ensures that you'll have the resources you need tomorrow.

How to Build Long-Term Savings

Building long-term savings is a gradual process that requires discipline, patience, and consistency. The sooner you begin, the more time your money has to grow, especially if you're investing it. Here are some ways to build long-term savings:

1. **Start Early**: The earlier you begin saving, the more time you give your money to grow. Time is one of the biggest advantages you have when it comes to saving for the long term, as your money can earn interest or dividends, and compound over time.
2. **Set Clear, Achievable Goals**: Whether you're saving for retirement, a house, or other long-term goals, setting clear, measurable goals helps you stay on track. Determine how much you need to save and by when, and break that down into monthly or yearly targets.
3. **Invest Regularly**: If you're investing for long-term growth, make contributions regularly. Set up automatic transfers into your retirement accounts, brokerage accounts, or other investment vehicles so you're consistently putting money toward your future.
4. **Take Advantage of Employer Contributions**: If your employer offers a **401(k)** match, take full advantage of it. This is essentially free money that will help you grow your retirement savings. Even if you can't contribute the maximum amount, contribute enough to take advantage of the employer match.
5. **Stay Consistent, Even with Small Amounts**: You don't have to start with large amounts to build long-term savings. Even small, regular contributions will add up over time, especially if you're investing. The key is to be consistent and allow your money to grow gradually.
6. **Diversify Your Investments**: Diversification is key to managing risk in your long-term savings. Spread your investments across different asset classes, such as stocks, bonds, and real estate, to protect your portfolio

from the ups and downs of the market.

Savings Accounts

A **general savings account** is one of the most basic types of savings accounts available at banks or credit unions. It's a secure place to store money you don't need to access right away but still want to keep safe and easily accessible. While a general savings account doesn't offer the high returns you might get from other investment options, it serves an important purpose—providing a stable and low-risk place to save for both short-term and long-term goals.

How General Savings Accounts Work

A general savings account is straightforward. You deposit money into the account, and in return, the bank pays you interest on the balance. The interest earned is usually lower than other types of investment accounts but still provides some growth for your savings.

The key advantage of a general savings account is liquidity. **Liquidation** means withdrawing money from your account and turning it into cash. For example, if you have $500 in your savings account and decide to take it out to pay for something, you're liquidating your savings. You're converting the money in your account into cash that you can use. If you need to withdraw your money for an emergency or other expenses, you can do so without penalty (although there may be limits on the number of withdrawals you can make each month). This makes it a great option for storing funds you may need soon but don't want to keep in your checking account where it could be spent easily.

Benefits of a General Savings Account

There are several benefits to using a general savings account:

1. **Safety**: One of the biggest advantages of a general savings account is

the safety it offers. Banks and credit unions typically insure deposits up to $250,000 through the **Federal Deposit Insurance Corporation (FDIC)** for banks or **National Credit Union Administration (NCUA)** for credit unions. This means that even if the bank or credit union were to fail, your money is protected.

2. **Low Risk**: General savings accounts are low-risk. The money in your account is not subject to market fluctuations like investments in stocks or bonds. The downside is that the interest earned is usually lower than that of other investment accounts, but it remains a safe place to store your funds.

3. **Easy Access**: If you need to access your savings, general savings accounts make it easy. Most banks offer online banking, ATMs, or even in-person branch services for withdrawals. While there may be some limits on how many withdrawals you can make per month, your money is readily available when you need it.

4. **Automatic Transfers**: General savings accounts can be a helpful tool for building savings with little effort. You can set up automatic transfers from your checking account to your savings account each month. This means you're consistently putting money aside without having to think about it.

Saving Money with Interest: How Your Savings Can Grow

When you save money, it's not just about putting it aside—it's about making your money work for you. A **savings account** allows you to do just that by earning **interest** on the money you deposit. Interest is essentially the bank paying you for letting them hold onto your money, and over time, this interest can help your savings grow without you having to do anything extra. Whether you're building an emergency fund or saving for a future goal, understanding how savings accounts work and how interest helps your money grow can make a big difference in reaching your financial goals faster. In this section, we'll explore how savings accounts earn interest and how you can take advantage of them to make your money work harder for you.

Types of Savings Accounts That Earn Interest

There are different types of savings accounts that offer varying interest rates, so it's important to choose the right one for your needs. Some common types include:

- **Basic Savings Accounts**: These accounts are easy to open, have no risk, and provide a safe place for your money. They usually offer low interest rates.
- **High-Yield Savings Accounts**: These accounts offer higher interest rates than basic savings accounts. The higher the interest rate, the more your money will grow. High-yield savings accounts are perfect for people who want to earn more interest on their savings while keeping their money safe and easily accessible.
- **Money Market Accounts**: A money market account is similar to a savings account but typically offers higher interest rates. Some money market accounts also provide check-writing capabilities and debit card access, though they may require a higher minimum balance.

While general savings accounts are low-risk, they typically offer lower interest rates than other types of savings or investment accounts. Interest rates can vary significantly from one bank to another, and the rate is often lower than rates for high-yield savings accounts.

In general, the interest rate on a savings account may be as low as a few tenths of a percent—sometimes as low as 0.01% or 0.05%. This means that for every $1,000 you save, you could earn as little as $0.10 to $5 in interest over the course of a year. While this isn't much, it's still more than you'd earn by keeping the money in cash under your mattress, and it allows your savings to grow, even if just a little bit.

Simple vs. Compound Interest: How Your Savings Can Grow

When you save money in a bank account or invest in different financial products, you're often paid **interest**—this is the money the bank or institution gives you for allowing them to use your funds. There are two main ways interest can be earned: **simple interest** and **compound interest**. Both are important to understand, as they affect how much your money grows over time.

Simple interest is calculated only on the original amount of money you save or invest. It's straightforward and easy to understand. On the other hand, **compound interest** allows you to earn interest on both the money you originally deposited and the interest that has already been added to your account. This can cause your savings to grow much faster over time.

Simple Interest: How Interest Works on Your Original Deposit

Simple interest is a way of calculating how much money you can earn on your savings or investment based only on the initial amount of money you deposit, also known as the principal. Unlike compound interest, simple interest doesn't consider any interest earned on the money that has already been added to your account. Instead, you only earn interest on your original deposit for the entire length of the investment or savings period.

Imagine you lend a friend $100, and they agree to pay you 10% interest on that loan every year. If you keep the $100 loaned to them for 3 years, here's how simple interest works:

- Each year, you'll earn 10% of $100, which is $10.
- After the first year, you get $10 in interest, so your total is $110 ($100 + $10).
- After the second year, you earn another $10 in interest, making it $120.
- After the third year, you earn another $10, so now you have $130.

At the end of 3 years, you'll have $130 in total: your original $100 plus $30 in interest ($10 for each of the 3 years). The interest was always calculated on the original $100, not the interest you earned in the previous years, which is what makes it simple interest.

Compound Interest: How Your Money Grows Faster

Compound interest is one of the most powerful tools you can use to grow your savings. It's the process where you earn interest not only on the money you initially save, but also on the interest that has already been added to your account. This means that your money starts working harder for you over time, growing faster than with simple interest alone.

What is Compound Interest?

To understand compound interest, let's break it down:

- **Interest** is the money you earn on the money you've saved or invested. When you put your money into a savings account, the bank pays you interest to thank you for letting them hold onto it.
- **Compound interest** means that the interest you earn gets added to the amount of money you have saved, and then you start earning interest on that new, larger amount.

So, instead of just earning interest on the money you originally saved (which is called the principal), you also earn interest on the interest. Over time, this makes your savings grow faster than if you were only earning interest on the original amount.

Imagine you invest $100 in an account that offers 10% compound interest annually for 3 years. With compound interest, you earn interest not just on your initial deposit, but also on the interest that gets added to your account each year.

Here's how it works:

- **Year 1**: You start with $100. At the end of the year, you earn 10% interest, which is $10. Now, your total balance is $110 ($100 + $10).

54

- **Year 2**: In the second year, you earn 10% interest on the new total of $110, not just the original $100. 10% of $110 is $11. Now, your balance is $121 ($110 + $11).
- **Year 3**: In the third year, you earn 10% interest on the new total of $121. 10% of $121 is $12.10. Now, your balance is $133.10 ($121 + $12.10).
- At the end of 3 years, you'll have $133.10—your original $100 plus $33.10 in interest. The difference between simple and compound interest is that with compound interest, the interest you earn each year gets added to your total balance, so you earn interest on your interest, which makes your savings grow faster over time.

As you can see, the interest keeps getting bigger each year because you're earning interest on both your original money and the interest you earned in the past. This is **compounding**—it's like your interest is earning its own interest.

Why Is Compound Interest So Powerful?

The main reason compound interest is so powerful is because of time. The longer your money is left to grow, the more it will grow. This is why it's best to start saving as early as possible. The more time your money has to earn interest on both the principal and the interest, the more your savings can grow.

Let's look at the same example over a longer period of time:

- **After 10 years**: You would have $1,628.89, nearly $630 more than your original $1,000.
- **After 20 years**: You would have $2,653.30, more than double your original savings.

The longer your money stays in an account earning compound interest, the more dramatic the growth.

The Key Ingredients for Compound Interest:

1. **Interest Rate**: The higher the interest rate, the faster your money will grow. If you earn 5% interest, your money grows at a certain rate, but if the interest rate were 10%, it would grow twice as fast.
2. **Time**: The longer you leave your money invested or saved, the more time it has to grow. This is why it's so important to start saving early!
3. **Frequency of Compounding**: Compound interest doesn't happen just once a year. It can happen multiple times per year (monthly, quarterly, etc.). The more often interest is added to your account, the faster your money grows. If your interest is compounded monthly, your savings will grow faster than if it's compounded just once per year.

Compound Interest in the Real World

You can find compound interest in many places:

- **Savings accounts**: Many banks offer compound interest on savings, which means the money you put into your account grows over time.
- **Investments**: When you invest in stocks, bonds, or mutual funds, the money you earn from those investments (like dividends or capital gains) can also earn compound interest if you reinvest it.
- **Retirement accounts**: If you save in a 401(k) or IRA for retirement, compound interest helps your money grow over the decades until you need it.

Compound interest is one of the most powerful tools for growing your savings. It helps your money grow faster by allowing you to earn interest on the interest you've already earned. The earlier you start saving and the longer you leave your money to grow, the more it will multiply. By understanding and taking advantage of compound interest, you can reach your financial goals much faster and build wealth over time.

Retirement Accounts

When it comes to saving for the future, especially for when you're no longer working, retirement accounts are one of the best tools to help you build wealth over time. They are special accounts that offer tax benefits, meaning they help you save money while reducing your tax bills. While retirement might seem like a long way off, the sooner you start saving, the more money you can build over time. Let's break down the most common types of retirement accounts to help you understand how they work.

401(k) Plans

A **401(k)** is a retirement account offered by many employers. It lets you save money directly from your paycheck before you even see it. This means the money you put into your 401(k) is not taxed until you take it out later, usually after you retire. Many employers will even match a portion of what you contribute. So if you put in $100, your employer might add another $50 or $100. This is like getting free money for saving!

401(k)s are usually a great option because your employer is helping you save. However, the money you put in can only be used when you retire, so it's important to think of it as a long-term savings account. You can choose how to invest the money in your 401(k), but keep in mind that there may be rules about when and how you can withdraw the funds.

Traditional IRA

An **IRA** stands for Individual Retirement Account. A **Traditional IRA** is a type of IRA where the money you contribute is tax-deductible. This means that when you put money into a Traditional IRA, you don't pay taxes on that money right away. Instead, you'll pay taxes when you take the money out during retirement.

One advantage of a Traditional IRA is that you can open one on your own, even if your employer doesn't offer a 401(k) plan. The downside is that you have a limit on how much you can contribute each year, and once you start taking money out, you'll have to pay taxes on it.

Roth IRA

A **Roth IRA** works a bit differently. Instead of getting a tax break when you put money in, you pay taxes on the money you contribute up front. But here's the big advantage: when you take money out during retirement, you don't have to pay taxes on it at all, which can save you a lot of money in the future.

Roth IRAs also let you take out your contributions (the money you put in) anytime, without penalty, but the earnings (the money your savings make) should stay in the account until you're at least 59½ years old. Roth IRAs are a great choice if you think you'll be in a higher tax bracket when you retire.

Choosing the Right Retirement Account

Each type of retirement account has its own pros and cons, but the main thing to remember is that they are all designed to help you save for the future. The best option depends on your personal situation, such as whether your employer offers a 401(k) plan or how much you can afford to save.

- If your employer offers a 401(k) and matches your contributions, it's a great idea to take advantage of that "free money."
- If you don't have a 401(k) plan, a Traditional IRA or Roth IRA can be a good way to start saving on your own.

The key to building wealth for the future is to start saving early, no matter which retirement account you choose. The sooner you start, the more your money can grow over time, helping you secure a comfortable future when you're ready to retire.

Health Savings Accounts (HSAs): A Smart Way to Save for Medical Expenses

A Health Savings Account (HSA) is a special type of savings account designed to help you pay for healthcare expenses while offering significant tax advantages. Unlike regular savings accounts, HSAs are specifically tailored to cover medical costs, from doctor's visits to prescription medications and even some procedures not covered by traditional insurance plans. HSAs are especially beneficial if you have a high-deductible health plan (HDHP), but they can be a great tool for anyone looking to save money on healthcare and reduce their taxable income.

How an HSA Works

To open an HSA, you must have a high-deductible health plan (HDHP), which is a health insurance plan with a higher deductible than typical plans. The benefit of an HDHP is that you pay lower monthly premiums, which makes it more affordable than traditional plans. However, the higher deductible means you'll need to pay more out-of-pocket before your insurance kicks in. That's where the HSA comes in.

You can contribute money to your HSA tax-free, and the funds can be used for eligible medical expenses without paying taxes when you withdraw them. This triple-tax advantage is what makes an HSA so attractive:

- **Tax-deductible contributions**: The money you contribute to your HSA is deducted from your taxable income for the year, which lowers your overall tax bill. For example, if you contribute $3,000 to your HSA, your taxable income for the year is reduced by that amount, meaning you pay less in taxes.
- **Tax-free growth**: The money in your HSA grows without being taxed, much like how money in a 401(k) grows for retirement.
- **Tax-free withdrawals**: When you use the funds to pay for qualified medical expenses, you won't pay taxes on the money you take out.

Eligible Expenses for an HSA

HSAs can be used to cover a wide range of medical expenses, both for you and your dependents. Some examples of qualified expenses include:

- Doctor visits, hospital care, and surgeries
- Prescription medications
- Dental care, such as cleanings, fillings, and braces
- Vision care, including eyeglasses, contact lenses, and LASIK surgery
- Mental health services and therapy
- Over-the-counter medications (with a prescription)
- Health-related products, like bandages and first-aid supplies

You can use your HSA funds to pay for these expenses at any time, and as long as you follow the rules, your withdrawals will be tax-free.

Benefits of Having an HSA

An HSA offers several benefits, especially when compared to other savings accounts or healthcare options:

1. **Tax Savings**: The combination of tax-deductible contributions, tax-free growth, and tax-free withdrawals makes the HSA one of the best tools for saving on healthcare expenses.
2. **Rollover Year-to-Year**: Unlike flexible spending accounts (FSAs), which require you to use the funds by the end of the year or lose them, HSAs allow you to roll over any unused funds into the next year. There's no "use-it-or-lose-it" rule, so you can keep the money in your account and let it grow for future medical expenses, even into retirement.
3. **Retirement Savings Potential**: While HSAs are designed for healthcare costs, they can also serve as a retirement savings tool. After age 65, you can withdraw money from your HSA for any reason, not just medical expenses, and you'll only pay regular income taxes (like you would

on a traditional IRA or 401(k)). This makes HSAs a great addition to your retirement planning, especially if you've already maxed out contributions to other retirement accounts.

4. **Lower Healthcare Costs**: By using HSA funds for eligible medical expenses, you're avoiding the need to use other savings or credit cards, which can lead to debt. You also don't have to pay taxes on your healthcare withdrawals, which means you get more value for your money.

Contribution Limits for an HSA

Each year, the government sets limits on how much you can contribute to your HSA. Be sure to check your HSA records for the year in which you used it, as this will help you keep track of your contributions, withdrawals, and any qualified medical expenses. Keeping an accurate record will ensure that you follow the rules and maximize the tax benefits of your HSA, while also helping you stay organized for tax reporting and future savings. These limits are set to ensure that people with high-deductible health plans are able to save enough to cover their out-of-pocket medical expenses, but they also prevent HSA holders from contributing excessive amounts.

How to Maximize Your HSA

To get the most out of your HSA, it's important to treat it as both a healthcare savings account and a long-term investment tool. Here's how you can maximize its benefits:

1. **Contribute the Maximum**: Try to contribute as much as you can to your HSA each year, up to the allowed limit. This helps you build a significant balance that can grow over time.
2. **Invest the Funds**: Many HSA providers offer investment options, allowing you to invest the money in your account in stocks, bonds, or mutual funds. Since HSAs can be used for long-term savings, investing

your funds allows them to grow much faster than if they were kept in a cash savings account. The earlier you start investing, the more time your money has to grow.

3. **Use Other Funds for Immediate Medical Expenses**: If you can afford to, pay for your current medical expenses out of pocket and let your HSA funds grow for the future. By doing this, you can allow the money in your HSA to accumulate, taking advantage of the tax-free growth.

4. **Save for Retirement Healthcare**: While HSAs are great for covering immediate medical costs, they can also help with healthcare expenses in retirement. Health care costs tend to rise as we get older, and having a fully funded HSA in retirement can help cover those expenses without burdening your other retirement accounts.

When to Use Your HSA

It's important to use your HSA wisely. If you're in a position to pay out-of-pocket for medical expenses, consider letting your HSA funds grow by leaving them untouched. However, if you're faced with high medical bills, your HSA is there to help you cover those costs tax-free. The flexibility of the HSA gives you control over how and when you use it.

An HSA is a powerful tool for saving on healthcare expenses, and it offers significant tax advantages that can help you build long-term wealth for medical needs and beyond. By contributing regularly, investing your funds, and using your HSA strategically, you can enjoy the benefits of tax-free growth and prepare for both present and future healthcare costs. Whether you're saving for current medical expenses or planning for retirement, an HSA can be a valuable part of your overall financial strategy.

Chapter 5

Increasing Your Income: Unlocking More Financial Opportunities

"Twenty years from now you will be more disappointed by the things that you didn't do than by the ones you did do. So throw off the bowlines. Sail away from the safe harbor. Catch the trade winds in your sails. Explore. Dream. Discover." -
Mark Twain

While saving money is a powerful way to build wealth, another option to improve your financial situation is to **increase your income**. By finding ways to earn more money, you can reach your financial goals faster and have more flexibility to save or invest. Whether through a side hustle, asking for a raise, or exploring new job opportunities, increasing your income gives you more resources to put toward savings, debt repayment, or other financial goals. Let's explore some ways you can boost your income and take control of your financial future.

Side Hustles and Freelancing

One of the most popular ways to increase your income is by starting a **side hustle** or **freelance work**. A side hustle is any job or business you take on in addition to your primary source of income. This can be anything from freelancing in your area of expertise (such as writing, graphic design, or tutoring) to starting a small business (like an online store or offering services like dog walking or babysitting). Side hustles allow you to leverage your skills or interests to earn extra money on the side, often with flexible hours.

Asking for a Raise

If you're currently employed, one of the most direct ways to increase your income is to ask for a **raise**. If you've been performing well at your job and taking on additional responsibilities, your employer may be open to offering you a salary increase. Before asking for a raise, do some research to understand the average salary for your role and industry in your area. Prepare evidence of your achievements and contributions to the company to show why you deserve a raise.

Sometimes, the right timing and preparation can make all the difference, especially if your company is performing well financially. If a raise isn't possible, you could also ask for other benefits, like extra vacation days, flexible work hours, or a bonus structure.

Upgrading Your Skills or Education

Increasing your income isn't always just about getting a second job; it can also mean improving your skills or qualifications to earn a higher salary in your current field. Consider taking **online courses**, earning certifications, or gaining new skills that are in high demand in your industry. Websites like **Coursera** or **LinkedIn Learning** offer affordable courses in everything from business management to coding, marketing, and data science.

By upgrading your skills, you become more valuable to your current employer or more competitive when applying for higher-paying jobs. Investing in your education can provide long-term benefits that increase your earning potential significantly.

Starting a Small Business

If you have a passion or a skill you want to share with others, **starting your own business** could be a great way to increase your income. Whether it's offering services like graphic design or photography, starting an e-commerce store, or creating content like blogs or YouTube channels, a small business can grow into a substantial source of income over time.

Starting a business doesn't require a large investment, especially with the resources available online, and it can often be done on a part-time basis until it grows. Many entrepreneurs begin by offering their services to friends and family, then expand through word-of-mouth or online marketing.

Exploring New Job Opportunities

If you're finding it difficult to increase your income at your current job, it may be time to look for new opportunities. Changing jobs or industries can result in a significant salary boost, especially if you're moving into a high-demand field. Keep an eye on job openings and use platforms like **LinkedIn**, **Indeed**, and **Glassdoor** to search for positions that offer better pay, benefits, or career growth potential.

Sometimes, switching employers is one of the quickest ways to get a raise, especially if you've outgrown your current role. Employers are often willing to offer a higher salary to attract top talent.

Monetizing Hobbies or Passions

If you have hobbies or interests that you're passionate about, you can turn them into income-generating opportunities. For example, if you enjoy crafting, you can sell your creations on platforms like **Etsy**. If you love fitness, consider becoming a fitness trainer or teaching yoga. If you're a good cook or baker, offering catering services or baking for local events can also be a profitable side venture.

Turning your passion into a part-time business not only increases your income but also makes work feel more fulfilling. Plus, it often offers the flexibility to work around your schedule.

Renting Out Assets

If you own property or valuable items, you can make money by renting them out. This could include:

- **Renting out a room** in your home or even your entire house on platforms like **Airbnb**.
- **Renting out your car** through services like **Turo**.
- **Renting equipment** like cameras, tools, or camping gear when you're not using them.

These options allow you to leverage assets you already own to earn additional income with minimal effort.

Passive Income Streams

Another way to increase your income is by creating **passive income** streams. This type of income comes from sources where you do the work upfront, and then the money continues to come in with little ongoing effort. Examples include:

- **Rental Income**: If you own real estate, renting out property can provide regular income.
- **Dividend Stocks**: Some stocks pay out dividends regularly, providing you with a stream of income from the companies you own shares in.
- **Creating Digital Products**: If you have expertise in a particular area, you could create and sell digital products like e-books, online courses, or printables that can generate income without much effort after the initial creation.

It's important to note that **passive income** doesn't always mean **hands-off**. While the idea of earning money with minimal effort is appealing, many passive income streams still require some initial work, time, or investment before they start generating revenue. While passive income requires some upfront time, effort, or investment, it can provide ongoing income over time with less active involvement.

Cutting Expenses to Free Up More Money

Increasing your income isn't the only way to improve your financial situation. **Cutting back on unnecessary expenses** is another way to free up more money to save, invest, or pay off debt. Consider reviewing your budget to see where you can cut costs:

- **Cancel unused subscriptions**: Streaming services, magazines, or gym memberships that aren't being used can be eliminated. Use your new found time to learn a new skill.
- **Refinance loans**: If you have loans with high-interest rates, look into refinancing them to reduce your monthly payments and save money over time.
- **Switch to cheaper alternatives**: Look for ways to reduce everyday costs, like switching to generic brands, cooking at home more often, or using coupons.

By cutting back on non-essential spending, you can effectively increase your disposable income and use it more strategically to achieve your financial goals.

Networking and Building Relationships

Sometimes, increasing your income can come from **building relationships** and networking with others. By connecting with professionals in your field or related industries, you may discover new opportunities for work, side gigs, or business partnerships. Networking can open doors to higher-paying roles, collaborations, or even job offers that you may not find through traditional job-search methods.

Leveraging the Gig Economy

The gig economy offers flexible opportunities to earn money on your own schedule. Platforms like **Uber**, **Lyft**, **DoorDash**, **Instacart**, and **TaskRabbit** allow you to use your spare time to earn extra income by driving, delivering groceries, or completing tasks for others. These gigs can be a great way to make extra money if you have time outside of your regular job.

Selling Unused Items

If you have unused or unwanted items around your house, consider selling them to raise extra cash. Whether it's clothes, electronics, furniture, or collectibles, platforms like **eBay**, **Facebook Marketplace**, and **Poshmark** make it easy to sell things you no longer need. Not only can this help you declutter, but it can also generate extra income with minimal effort.

Investing in Yourself

Sometimes the best investment you can make is in your own personal development. Investing time or money into improving your skills, knowledge, or health can increase your earning potential in the long run. Whether it's through formal education, online courses, workshops, or coaching, enhancing your abilities can lead to higher-paying jobs, new career opportunities, and even business success.

Selling Creative Work or Art

If you're creative, there are numerous platforms where you can sell your artwork, photography, music, or crafts. Platforms like **Etsy**, **Redbubble**, and **Society6** provide an opportunity to sell your designs, prints, music, and more. If you're good at a craft, photography, or other artistic endeavors, this could be a lucrative way to turn your hobbies into income.

Peer-to-Peer Lending

Another option to earn money is by participating in **peer-to-peer lending**. This involves lending money to individuals or businesses through platforms like **LendingClub** or **Prosper**. You earn interest on the money you lend, similar to how a bank would. However, lending money to others carries risks, so it's important to research the platforms and understand the risks involved before lending your money.

By combining several of these income-boosting strategies, you can diversify your sources of income and improve your financial situation faster. Whether you're working on a side hustle, looking to upgrade your skills, or finding new ways to make passive income, increasing your income is a powerful tool for achieving your financial goals. The key is to identify opportunities that align with your skills, interests, and available time so that you can make the most of your efforts and build long-term wealth.

Increasing your income is one of the best ways to take control of your financial future. Whether through side hustles, asking for a raise, upgrading your skills, or starting your own business, there are countless opportunities to earn more money and build wealth. The key is finding the right option for your skills, interests, and available time. By increasing your income, you can speed up the process of achieving your financial goals, giving you more freedom and opportunities for the future.

Chapter 6

Understanding Credit and How It Can Boost Your Financial Confidence

"Formal education will make you a living; self-education will make you a fortune."
- Jim Rohn

When it comes to managing money, understanding **credit** is one of the most important aspects of your financial life. Whether you're trying to buy a home, purchase a car, or even build a successful business, your credit will play a significant role in helping you get there. But if you're like many people who never had a strong foundation in financial literacy, credit can seem like a confusing or intimidating topic.

In this chapter, we'll break down the concept of credit, explain how it works, and show you how having good credit can boost your financial confidence and open doors to better financial opportunities. Understanding credit will not only help you make smarter financial decisions but will also empower you to take control of your financial future.

What is Credit?

Credit is the ability to borrow money or access goods and services with the understanding that you will pay for them later, usually with interest. For example, when you get a credit card, you're borrowing money from the credit card company, and you agree to pay it back later. The amount of credit you can borrow is usually based on your creditworthiness, which is determined by your **credit score**.

Your credit score is a numerical representation of your ability to repay borrowed money. The higher your score, the more trustworthy you are to lenders. This score helps lenders determine whether they should give you a loan or a credit card, and it can also affect the interest rate you'll be charged. The better your credit, the more likely you are to receive loans with favorable terms—like lower interest rates—which can save you money in the long run.

How Credit Works

Credit allows you to borrow money with the expectation that you'll pay it back over time. When you use credit, whether through a credit card, loan, or other financial product, you're borrowing money that you'll pay back in installments or a lump sum.

Credit Reports

Your **credit report** is a detailed summary of your credit history, showing how well you've managed credit in the past. It includes information about your **loans, credit cards, payment history**, and **credit inquiries**. Lenders, landlords, and even employers may review your credit report when making decisions about you.

- **How to access it**: You're entitled to one free credit report per year from each of the three major credit bureaus—**Equifax, Experian**, and **TransUnion**—via the official website, **AnnualCreditReport.com**.

- **What's included**: Your credit report will show details such as your credit card accounts, loans, payment history, public records (like bankruptcies), and any recent credit inquiries.
- **Why it's important**: Regularly reviewing your credit report ensures there are no mistakes or fraudulent activity that could hurt your credit score.

Credit Inquiries (Hard vs. Soft Inquiries)

Every time you apply for credit, such as a loan or a new credit card, it results in a **credit inquiry**. These inquiries can affect your credit score, depending on the type:

- **Hard Inquiry**: This occurs when a lender checks your credit report as part of their decision-making process (e.g., applying for a mortgage, car loan, or credit card). Hard inquiries can cause a small, temporary drop in your score. However, too many hard inquiries in a short period can be seen as a red flag to lenders, indicating that you may be over-extending yourself.
- **Soft Inquiry**: This occurs when you check your own credit report or when a company checks your credit for purposes like pre-approving you for offers. Soft inquiries do not affect your credit score.

Understanding the difference helps you be mindful of how often you apply for credit and the potential impact it could have on your score.

Credit Utilization: Keeping Your Spending in Check

Credit utilization is simply the amount of money you're using from your total available credit. It's an important factor in your credit score because it shows how much of your available credit you're actually using. The general rule is that the lower your credit utilization, the better it is for your credit score.

Here's an example to make it clearer:

Let's say you have a credit card with a $1,000 credit limit. If you're using $300 of that limit, your credit utilization is 30% ($300 divided by $1,000). This is a healthy level. But if you're using $800, your credit utilization is 80%, which is considered high.

High credit utilization can lower your credit score because it may signal to lenders that you're depending too much on credit. They might see you as a risk because it looks like you could struggle to pay off what you owe.

To keep your credit score healthy, aim to use **less than 30%** of your available credit. If you can keep it even lower, like under 10%, that's even better for your score.

How to Keep Your Credit Utilization Low

- **Pay off balances quickly**: Try to pay off your credit card balances in full each month. This keeps your utilization low and avoids interest charges.
- **Request a credit limit increase**: If you can't pay down your balance quickly, you might want to ask your credit card issuer for a higher credit limit. This can lower your utilization ratio because the more available credit you have, the less you're using in comparison.
- **Use multiple cards**: If you have more than one credit card, spreading out your purchases between cards can help keep the balance on each card low, which keeps your overall credit utilization in a good range.
- In short, managing your credit utilization wisely helps your credit score and makes you appear more responsible to lenders. The goal is to use credit in a way that shows you're in control, not relying on it too heavily.

Credit Limits

Your **credit limit** is the maximum amount of money you can borrow on your credit card or line of credit. Lenders determine your credit limit based on factors like your income, credit history, and creditworthiness.

- **How it impacts you**: A higher credit limit can help improve your credit utilization ratio if you keep your spending low. However, a higher limit also means you have more access to credit, so it's important to manage your spending responsibly.
- **Requesting a limit increase**: If you have a history of responsible credit use, you might be able to request a higher limit, which can improve your utilization ratio and possibly boost your credit score.

Types of Credit Accounts

There are various types of **credit accounts** that can appear on your credit report, and how you manage them influences your score. These include:

- **Revolving Credit**: This type of credit allows you to borrow up to a certain limit, repay it, and borrow again. **Credit cards** are the most common example. Managing revolving credit responsibly means making timely payments and keeping credit utilization low.
- **Installment Credit**: This is when you borrow a specific amount of money and agree to repay it in fixed installments. Examples include **auto loans**, **student loans**, and **mortgages**. Paying these off consistently and on time will positively impact your credit score.
- **Open Credit**: Open accounts require full payment every month, with no interest charged if paid off on time. **Charge cards** (like some American Express cards) are examples. Late payments or failure to pay the balance in full can hurt your score.

Having a mix of different types of credit accounts, when managed responsibly, can improve your credit score by showing you're capable of handling various forms of credit.

Payment History

Your **payment history** is one of the most important factor affecting your credit score, making up about 35% of the total score calculation. It shows whether you've paid your bills on time or if there have been late payments, defaults, or bankruptcies.

- **Why it's important**: On-time payments help build your credit history and show that you can manage debt responsibly. Late payments, defaults, or bankruptcies will significantly hurt your score and stay on your credit report for years.
- **How to improve it**: Always make at least the minimum payment on time. If you've missed payments, focus on catching up and making consistent, on-time payments moving forward.

Credit History Length

The length of time you've been using credit, known as **credit history length**, makes up about 15% of your credit score. A longer credit history gives lenders more data to assess your reliability.

- **Why it matters**: The longer your credit history, the better. However, even if you're just starting to build credit, establishing a positive credit history can set you up for financial success. Keeping old accounts open (even if you don't use them regularly) can help improve this aspect of your score.

Dealing with Debt

Managing debt is a critical aspect of building and maintaining good credit. Being in debt doesn't necessarily mean you have bad credit, but how you manage it will directly affect your score.

- **Paying down high-interest debt**: Prioritize paying down high-interest credit cards first. This not only improves your credit score but also saves you money in the long run.
- **Debt consolidation**: If you have multiple high-interest debts, consolidating them into one loan with a lower interest rate can simplify payments and lower your overall debt load, helping to boost your credit score.

When it comes to understanding credit, there are several important aspects beyond just knowing your credit score and how it affects loans or credit cards. These factors help shape your overall financial health and creditworthiness.

Credit Cards

A **credit card** is one of the most common forms of credit. When you use a credit card, you're essentially borrowing money from the card issuer to make a purchase. The key things to remember about credit cards are:

- **Credit limit**: This is the maximum amount of money you can borrow using your credit card. If your limit is $1,000, for example, that means you can spend up to $1,000 that you need to pay back.
- **Minimum payment**: Every month, you'll receive a bill that shows how much you owe. The minimum payment is the smallest amount you can pay without being charged a late fee or damaging your credit score.
- **Interest rates**: If you don't pay off your balance in full, the credit card company charges you interest on the remaining amount. High interest rates can lead to debt quickly, which is why paying off your balance in full is always the best practice.

Using Credit Cards Responsibly

Credit cards can be a great tool to build credit and manage purchases, but they need to be used carefully to avoid debt and keep your credit score healthy. Here's how you can use credit cards responsibly:

1. Pay Your Bill on Time: Always make at least the minimum payment by the due date. Missing payments can hurt your credit score and result in late fees. Setting up automatic payments can help ensure you never forget to pay.

2. Pay Your Balance in Full: Ideally, pay off your entire balance each month to avoid paying interest. If you only make the minimum payment, you'll be charged interest on the remaining balance, which can add up quickly.

3. Keep Your Credit Utilization Low: Try to use less than 30% of your available credit. For example, if you have a $1,000 credit limit, aim to keep your balance below $300. High credit utilization can negatively affect your credit score.

4. Don't Overspend: Use your credit card for things you can afford to pay back. Avoid using credit to buy things you don't need or can't afford, as it can quickly lead to debt that's difficult to pay off.

5. Review Your Statements Regularly: Always check your credit card statements to make sure you're being charged correctly. If you spot any errors or unauthorized charges, report them right away.

By following these tips, you can use your credit card to help build your credit, earn rewards, and manage your finances—without falling into debt.

Credit Scores

Your **credit score** is a number that ranges from 300 to 850 and represents your creditworthiness. A higher score means you're a less risky borrower, and a lower score means you may have trouble getting credit or paying off debt.

Credit scores are broken down into categories:

- **Excellent (750 and above)**: You're likely to receive the best loan terms and lowest interest rates.
- **Good (700-749)**: You're considered a reliable borrower and can qualify for good loan terms.

- **Fair (650-699)**: You may be approved for credit, but with higher interest rates.
- **Poor (below 650)**: Lenders may see you as a high-risk borrower, and it may be harder to secure loans or credit cards.

Your credit score is determined by several factors, including:

- **Payment history**: Whether you've paid your bills on time.
- **Credit utilization**: The percentage of your available credit that you use. The lower, the better.
- **Length of credit history**: How long you've been using credit.
- **Types of credit**: The variety of credit accounts you have, such as credit cards, auto loans, or mortgages.
- **Recent inquiries**: How often you've applied for credit in recent months.

How Credit Affects Your Financial Confidence

Understanding and managing credit can have a huge impact on your financial confidence. Here's how:

1. **Better Access to Loans and Credit:** When you understand how credit works and build a good credit score, you're more likely to be approved for loans and credit cards. Having access to credit can give you the financial flexibility to make large purchases, like a home, car, or business investment. It also allows you to handle emergencies without scrambling to find cash. For example, if your car breaks down unexpectedly, having a credit card can help you pay for repairs while you figure out a longer-term solution.

2. **Lower Interest Rates:** A good credit score means you'll likely qualify for loans or credit cards with **lower interest rates**. Lower interest rates mean you'll pay less money over time for things like car loans, mortgages, or credit card balances. For example, a mortgage with a 4% interest rate is much cheaper than one with a 6% interest rate. This can save you

thousands of dollars in the long run, giving you more money to invest, save, or spend on other goals.

3. **Renting and Housing Opportunities:** A good credit score can also make it easier to secure a rental property or buy a home. Landlords and mortgage lenders typically check your credit report to assess how reliable you are with paying bills. If you have a good score, they're more likely to approve you for a lease or loan, and you may be able to negotiate better terms.

4. **Building Trust with Others:** Managing credit responsibly helps you build trust with others. Whether it's a lender, a landlord, or even an employer, a strong credit history shows that you're reliable and capable of handling your financial obligations. This trust can open doors to new opportunities and help you build a more stable financial future.

5. **Peace of Mind and Control:** Finally, understanding credit and having control over your credit situation gives you peace of mind. You no longer have to worry about being rejected for loans or feeling lost in financial decisions. When you understand how credit works, you can make informed decisions that support your goals and give you more confidence in your financial journey.

Building Good Credit

Building good credit doesn't happen overnight, but it is entirely possible if you follow these steps:

- **Pay bills on time**: Payment history is one of the most important factors in your credit score.
- **Keep credit card balances low**: Try to use less than 30% of your available credit.
- **Monitor your credit**: Regularly check your credit report to ensure there are no errors or fraudulent activities.
- **Avoid too many credit inquiries**: Every time you apply for credit, it can slightly lower your score.

Understanding credit is a key part of taking control of your financial future. By learning how credit works, improving your credit score, and using credit responsibly, you can unlock greater financial opportunities, reduce stress about your financial situation, and gain confidence in your ability to manage your money. Whether it's getting approved for loans with better terms or simply having the ability to manage emergencies with ease, mastering credit will give you the financial freedom and confidence to build the life you want.

Chapter 7

Investing Made Easy: Growing Your Money, One Step at a Time

"Compound interest is the eighth wonder of the world. She who understands it, earns it. She who doesn't, pays it." – Albert Einstein

Investing is one of the most effective ways to build wealth and achieve long-term financial security. While saving is important for immediate goals, investing allows you to grow your money over time, often at a much faster rate. By putting your money in the right investment vehicles, you can take advantage of compounding returns, diversification, and the power of the markets to reach your financial goals, whether it's retirement, buying a home, or building generational wealth.

In this chapter, we'll explore why investing in yourself is so valuable, how you can do it, and the many ways it can pay off in both your financial and personal life. Whether it's improving your skills, focusing on your health, or enhancing your mindset, investing in yourself provides you with the tools to succeed and thrive in both your career and life.

Types of Investments

There are many types of investments, each with its own set of risks and potential rewards. Understanding these options can help you choose the best investment strategy for your goals and risk tolerance.

Stocks

- **What Are Stocks?**: When you buy a stock, you're buying a small ownership share in a company. Stocks offer the potential for high returns, but they also come with higher risk since their value can fluctuate based on the company's performance and the market.
- **How Do They Work?**: The value of stocks can rise and fall depending on factors like a company's profits, industry trends, and market conditions. You can earn money from stocks in two ways: **capital gains** (selling the stock for more than you paid for it) and **dividends** (periodic payments from the company based on their profits).

Bonds

- **What Are Bonds?**: Bonds are essentially loans you give to a company or government, and in return, they promise to pay you interest over time. Bonds are considered safer than stocks, but they usually offer lower returns.
- **How Do They Work?**: When you purchase a bond, you're lending money to an entity (like a government or corporation). In return, they agree to pay you periodic interest and return your principal (the original amount you invested) at the end of the bond term.

Real Estate

- **What Is Real Estate Investment?**: Investing in real estate involves purchasing property—whether for rental income or to sell for a profit. Real estate is considered a tangible asset, and it can be a good long-term investment.
- **How Does It Work?**: You can invest in real estate directly by buying property, or indirectly through **Real Estate Investment Trusts (REITs)**,

which allow you to invest in a portfolio of real estate properties. Rental properties can generate income through rent, while properties you sell may appreciate over time.

Mutual Funds and Exchange-Traded Funds (ETFs)

- **What Are Mutual Funds and ETFs?**: These are pools of money from many investors that are used to buy a diversified collection of stocks, bonds, or other assets. **Mutual funds** are managed by professional managers, while **ETFs** typically track a specific index, like the S&P 500.
- **How Do They Work?**: Both mutual funds and ETFs allow you to invest in a broad range of assets without having to pick individual stocks or bonds. They offer **diversification**, which helps spread out risk. ETFs trade like stocks, while mutual funds are typically bought and sold at the end of the day at their net asset value (NAV).

Cryptocurrency

- **What Is Cryptocurrency?**: Cryptocurrency is a digital or virtual form of money that uses encryption for security. Bitcoin, Ethereum, and other cryptocurrencies are decentralized, meaning they are not controlled by any central bank or government.
- **How Does It Work?**: Cryptocurrencies can be bought and sold on exchanges, and they may appreciate in value based on demand, technological advancements, and market trends. However, the volatility and risks involved make cryptocurrencies a more speculative investment.

Risk vs. Reward: Understanding the Balance in Investing

In the world of investing, risk vs. reward is one of the most important concepts to understand. Simply put, **risk** is the chance that you might lose some or all of your money, while **reward** refers to the potential return or profit you can earn from your investment. In general, the higher the risk you take on, the higher the potential reward—this is often called the risk-reward tradeoff. Understanding this relationship helps you make informed decisions about where to invest your money and how much risk you're willing to tolerate.

One key concept in investing is understanding the relationship between risk and reward. Higher-risk investments, like stocks or cryptocurrencies, tend to offer the potential for higher returns, but they also come with the possibility of losing money. On the other hand, safer investments like bonds or savings accounts may offer lower returns, but they also carry less risk.

When choosing investments, it's important to consider your **risk tolerance**—how much risk you're willing to take based on your financial goals, timeline, and comfort level with market fluctuations. Younger investors often have a higher risk tolerance because they have more time to recover from potential losses, while those closer to retirement may prefer safer, more stable investments.

Your risk tolerance is your ability and willingness to take on risk. It's influenced by several factors, including your financial situation, goals, and personality. Some people are more comfortable with risk and can handle the ups and downs of the market, while others prefer the stability of low-risk investments.

To assess your risk tolerance, ask yourself:

- How long can I leave my money invested? (The longer you can leave it, the more risk you can afford.)
- How would I feel if my investments lost value in the short term? (Being comfortable with short-term losses is important for long-term investing.)
- What are my financial goals? (Aggressive growth targets might require taking on more risk, while preserving wealth may require lower-risk investments.)

How to Get Started with Investing

If you're new to investing, it's important to start small and learn as you go. Here are some steps to help you get started:

1. **Set Your Goals**: Determine what you're investing for—whether it's retirement, a big purchase, or wealth building. This will guide your investment decisions.
2. **Open an Investment Account**: To buy stocks, bonds, or mutual funds, you'll need to open an investment account. This could be a **brokerage account** or a **retirement account** like an IRA or 401(k).
3. **Start with Low-Cost Investments**: If you're new to investing, consider starting with diversified funds, like ETFs or mutual funds, which give you exposure to a broad range of assets with lower risk.
4. **Invest Regularly**: Rather than trying to time the market, it's often better to invest consistently over time (known as **dollar-cost averaging**). This helps smooth out market fluctuations and reduces the risk of investing a large sum all at once.
5. **Learn and Adjust**: Investing is a long-term commitment, so it's important to educate yourself, stay informed, and adjust your investments as your financial situation and goals evolve.

The Best Investment You Can Make Is in Yourself

When it comes to building wealth and improving your financial situation, the best investment you can make is often not in stocks, bonds, or real estate—but in **yourself**. Investing in your own personal growth, skills, and knowledge can have a lasting impact on your future and is often the most rewarding investment you can make. Unlike other forms of investment, which may carry some level of risk or uncertainty, investing in yourself offers the potential for guaranteed returns, whether that's through higher earning potential, better job opportunities, or improved personal satisfaction.

Why Invest in Yourself?

The reason investing in yourself is the best decision you can make is simple: it increases your value in the marketplace, boosts your confidence, and helps you achieve your long-term goals. Whether it's gaining new skills, furthering your education, or improving your health, every effort you make to better yourself compounds over time, just like compound interest. The knowledge, skills, and habits you develop today can have a profound impact on your financial future tomorrow.

For example, learning a new skill, taking a certification course, or even improving your communication abilities can open doors to new job opportunities, promotions, or side gigs. Unlike financial investments, which may be subject to market risk, your personal growth provides a stable foundation for continued success. The time and energy you put into your personal development will pay off, often in ways that exceed the initial investment.

Types of Self-Investment

There are many ways you can invest in yourself. Some of the most impactful areas include:

- **Education and Skills Development**: Continuing to learn and grow through formal education, online courses, certifications, or self-study is one of the most powerful ways to invest in yourself. By enhancing your skills, you increase your earning potential and set yourself up for future career opportunities.
- **Physical Health**: Maintaining a healthy lifestyle—eating well, exercising regularly, and getting enough sleep—directly impacts your energy levels, focus, and productivity. When you invest in your health, you not only feel better but also have more energy to pursue your goals.
- **Mental and Emotional Health**: Taking care of your mental health is just as important as physical health. This could involve practicing mindfulness, therapy, stress management techniques, or simply taking

time for self-care. A healthy mind is crucial for success, resilience, and well-being.

- **Networking and Relationships**: Building meaningful relationships with others can provide personal and professional growth opportunities. Networking can help you find mentors, learn from others, and potentially discover career-changing opportunities. Strengthening your relationships also provides emotional support, which is invaluable during challenging times.
- **Financial Literacy and Money Management**: Understanding how money works, how to manage it, and how to make smart financial decisions is a powerful form of self-investment. Whether you take a class in personal finance, read books, or work with a financial advisor, becoming financially literate empowers you to make better choices with your money and build long-term wealth.

How to Start Investing in Yourself

The first step in investing in yourself is recognizing your strengths and areas where you can improve. Take stock of where you are and where you want to go. Do you want to develop a new career path? Are you looking to improve your health? Do you want to become better at managing your finances? Setting clear, actionable goals will help guide you in making the right investments.

Once you've identified areas for growth, here's how you can begin:

- **Set clear goals**: Whether you're learning a new skill, improving your health, or increasing your financial knowledge, setting specific and measurable goals will help you stay on track.
- **Dedicate time and resources**: Just like any investment, you need to commit time, energy, and possibly money to see results. For example, enrolling in a course, hiring a coach, or setting aside time for exercise will show your commitment to self-improvement.
- **Stay consistent**: Personal growth takes time. Just like compound interest,

the benefits of investing in yourself multiply over time. The more consistent you are, the greater the return on your investment.

- **Seek feedback and mentorship**: No one succeeds alone. Seek mentors who can guide you, provide constructive feedback, and help you grow. Learning from others' experiences can save you time and energy on your journey.

The Return on Investment

The return on investing in yourself can't always be measured in dollars and cents, but that doesn't make it any less valuable. The skills, knowledge, and habits you build can result in:

- Higher salaries and better job opportunities.
- Improved health, leading to more energy and a longer life.
- Greater emotional resilience and mental well-being.
- Personal fulfillment from pursuing your passions and goals.

Investing in yourself has a **compounding effect**. Just as compound interest grows your savings, the benefits of self-investment grow exponentially over time. The more you invest in your personal development today, the greater the returns you'll see in the future.

The best investment you can make is in yourself. By dedicating time, energy, and resources to personal growth, you set the foundation for greater success, happiness, and financial freedom. Whether it's improving your skills, enhancing your health, or learning more about money, every step you take toward investing in yourself brings you closer to your goals and helps you build a more fulfilling life. Start today, and watch how the returns pay off in the years to come.

The Power of Investment—In Money and Yourself

Investing, whether in financial assets or in yourself, is the key to long-term growth and success. While traditional investments like stocks, bonds, and real estate can help grow your wealth, the best investment you can make is in your own personal development. By improving your skills, health, and financial literacy, you build a foundation for greater opportunities, higher earning potential, and a more fulfilling life. Just like compound interest makes your money grow over time, investing in yourself compounds into greater returns, both personally and financially. The sooner you start investing—whether in assets or in your own growth—the more you stand to gain, both now and in the future.

Chapter 8

Entrepreneurship: Is Starting a Business the Right Move for You?

"Your most unhappy customers are your greatest source of learning." - *Bill Gates*

Entrepreneurship is often seen as an exciting way to take control of your financial future and achieve your goals, but it's important to understand that it's not for everyone. Starting and running a business requires hard work, persistence, and a willingness to take risks. While the rewards can be great, so can the challenges.

Being an entrepreneur means creating and running your own business. You make the decisions, take on the responsibilities, and are in charge of your own success or failure. Some people thrive in this environment, while others may find it overwhelming or stressful.

The Reality of Entrepreneurship

- **Risk and Uncertainty**: One of the biggest aspects of entrepreneurship is the **risk** involved. Starting a business often means putting your money, time, and energy into something that may not succeed. You may face long hours, financial strain, and uncertainty. Many entrepreneurs fail before they find success, so it's important to be prepared for setbacks.

- **Time and Effort**: Running a business requires a lot of **time** and **effort**. Entrepreneurs often work more than the typical 9-5 job, especially when starting out. You'll need to wear multiple hats: managing finances, marketing your business, handling customer service, and more.
- **Financial Investment**: Starting a business often requires upfront investment, whether it's your own savings, a loan, or outside investors. Not everyone has the resources or desire to take on this kind of financial responsibility.

Is Entrepreneurship Right for You?

Before deciding to start a business, it's important to reflect on whether entrepreneurship aligns with your personality, goals, and lifestyle. Entrepreneurship comes with its share of uncertainty and challenges, so consider whether you're willing to take on the risks involved. If you prefer stability and predictability, you might find the unpredictable nature of entrepreneurship stressful.

Starting and running a business requires a significant time commitment. It's not just about having the idea; it's about dedicating the time and energy to making it work. If you already have a full-time job or other personal commitments, like family responsibilities, you may find it difficult to manage the demands of building a business alongside those obligations.

Another key factor is how you handle setbacks and failure. Not every business succeeds, and there will be challenges along the way. If you're someone who gets discouraged easily or struggles with the possibility of failure, entrepreneurship could be tough for you. On the other hand, if you can bounce back from mistakes and see them as learning opportunities, it may be the right fit.

Successful entrepreneurs often have a strong passion or a particular skill they can turn into a business. It's important to ask yourself if there is something you're passionate about or a talent you can leverage in the market. If you have a deep interest in a product or service, along with the expertise to make it succeed, then entrepreneurship could be a great path to explore.

Generating Ideas for a Business

Coming up with the right business idea is one of the most exciting—and sometimes challenging—parts of entrepreneurship. The key is to find an idea that aligns with your passion, skills, and the needs of the market. A good business idea not only has the potential to succeed but also excites you and keeps you motivated.

Solving a Problem: The Foundation of a Successful Business Idea

At the heart of many successful businesses is the ability to **solve a problem**. In fact, the best business ideas often come from recognizing a need or challenge that people face, and then offering a solution that makes their lives easier, better, or more efficient. The reason businesses that solve real problems tend to thrive is because they provide value, and when you provide value, customers are more likely to pay for it.

When thinking about starting a business, consider problems you have personally encountered or problems that others may be dealing with on a larger scale. Identifying a problem and coming up with a solution is not just about offering a product or service—it's about filling a gap in the market where demand exists. Here's how solving a problem can lead to a thriving business:

Identifying Pain Points

To find a problem worth solving, you first need to identify **pain points**—specific issues, frustrations, or inconveniences that people experience in their day-to-day lives. Pain points can be big or small, but they are often the driving force behind new business ideas. These problems might be unique to a specific group, industry, or even to yourself.

For example:

- **Time Management**: Many people struggle to find enough time in the day to get everything done. A service or app that helps them better manage their schedules, track tasks, or stay focused could solve this problem.
- **Lack of Convenience**: If a particular product or service is inconvenient to use or hard to access, creating a more user-friendly version could address that pain. Think about how ride-sharing services like Uber solved the problem of waiting for a taxi.

By identifying common problems that people are willing to spend money to solve, you can create a business idea that offers a clear solution.

Understanding the Problem

Once you identify a pain point, it's important to deeply understand the problem you're trying to solve. Don't just assume you know the solution—spend time researching the issue, talking to people who experience it, and gathering feedback. This will give you a more accurate picture of the problem and allow you to create a solution that truly meets people's needs.

For example, if you're trying to solve the problem of managing household chores, simply creating an app won't be enough unless you understand what people actually need—whether it's reminders, shared lists, or scheduling help. Understanding the root cause of the problem ensures that the solution you create is relevant and effective.

Creating a Practical Solution

Once you've fully understood the problem, you can start to think about practical solutions. A great business idea often revolves around offering a simple, yet effective, solution to a problem. Your solution doesn't have to be complex or groundbreaking—it just needs to provide real value to the people facing the problem.

Let's say you notice that many people are frustrated with the complexity of cooking healthy meals at home. A business idea might be creating a subscription service that delivers healthy, pre-measured ingredients with easy-to-follow recipes. This solution addresses the problem of time constraints and the stress of meal planning while making healthy eating more accessible.

Testing Your Solution

Once you've come up with a solution, it's important to test it in the real world before fully committing. Creating a prototype or a minimum viable product (MVP) allows you to see if your solution actually works and if people are willing to pay for it.

For example, if you create a new app or product, launch it to a small group of users first and gather feedback. What works well? What could be improved? Testing your solution in the market can help you fine-tune it, adjust to customer needs, and ensure that it truly solves the problem in a way that resonates with your target audience.

Standing Out by Solving Problems in a New Way

Many successful businesses offer solutions to problems that have already been addressed by others, but they do so in a new or more efficient way. The key to standing out is to find a way to offer a better solution—whether that's through convenience, price, quality, or customer experience.

For example, while there were already food delivery services before **DoorDash**, they stood out by making the process faster, more user-friendly, and available in more places. They solved the problem of getting food delivered quickly and easily, providing more value than previous options.

Your business doesn't always have to be the first to solve a problem; it just needs to solve it in a way that customers will appreciate and be willing to pay for.

Adding Value Beyond the Problem

Sometimes, solving a problem can also mean adding value beyond the initial solution. Offering additional features, services, or ongoing support can make your business even more appealing to customers. For instance, a fitness app may help users track their workouts (solving the problem of staying on track), but adding personalized workout plans, progress tracking, or even a community feature can make your app even more valuable and keep users coming back.

The more value you can add, the more likely people will see your business as a solution they can't live without.

Scaling Your Solution

Once your solution is working and solving the problem effectively, the next step is **scaling**. This means expanding your business to reach more people or offering your solution in a broader way. Whether it's launching a new product, expanding to different markets, or offering new services, scaling your business allows you to reach more customers who need your solution.

If you've solved a problem in your local community, for example, you can scale it to a larger audience—either regionally, nationally, or even internationally. The more you can scale your business, the more potential it has to grow.

The Power of Problem-Solving in Business

At the heart of every great business is the ability to **solve a problem**. Whether you're providing a new product, a better service, or a more efficient way to accomplish something, solving problems that people care about will give you a competitive advantage. By focusing on understanding real needs, offering effective solutions, and constantly improving, your business can not only succeed but thrive. The most successful entrepreneurs know that by solving problems for others, they create value—and value is what drives business success.

Planning Your Business: Setting the Foundation for Success

Once you've identified a problem to solve and have a solution in mind, the next critical step is **planning your business**. A well-thought-out business plan is the foundation of any successful venture. It helps you stay focused, understand your market, and provide a roadmap for growing your business. Planning isn't just about writing down ideas; it's about organizing your thoughts, understanding your goals, and creating a strategy for execution.

Here's how to approach planning your business:

Define Your Business Idea Clearly

The first step in planning is to define your business idea clearly. What exactly are you offering, and how does it solve a problem? Be as specific as possible about your product or service and the target market you aim to serve. Ask yourself:

- What makes your business unique or different from others?
- Who are your potential customers, and what are their needs and pain points?
- How will your product or service benefit them?

This step helps solidify your concept and ensures you're offering something valuable to your customers.

Conduct Market Research

Before launching, it's crucial to understand your market—who your competitors are, what the demand is, and how you can stand out. Market research is the process of gathering information about your target audience, competitors, and industry trends.

You can conduct market research through surveys, talking to potential customers, or analyzing competitors' businesses. Consider questions like:

- Who are your competitors, and what are their strengths and weaknesses?
- What does your target market want, and how much are they willing to pay for it?
- What are the current trends in your industry that could affect your business?

By conducting research, you'll have a clearer understanding of your customers' needs, helping you adjust your offerings and approach.

Develop a Business Model

Your **business model** describes how your business will operate and generate revenue. It's essential to understand how your business will make money, and how much you'll charge for your product or service. There are many different models, and you can adjust them to fit your specific business. Some common business models include:

- **Subscription-based**: Customers pay a recurring fee for access to a product or service, such as streaming platforms or subscription boxes.
- **Freemium**: Offering a basic service for free while charging for premium features or content, like with many apps or software programs.
- **Retail**: Selling physical products either in-store or online.
- **Service-based**: Offering a service, such as consulting, coaching, or freelance work.

Once you decide on your model, you'll be able to determine pricing, profit margins, and sales strategies.

Set Clear Goals and Milestones

A business plan isn't just about the big picture—it's also about the smaller steps that will get you there. Set clear, **measurable goals** for your business, both short-term and long-term. These goals will guide your actions and keep you motivated as you build your business. Examples of goals might include:

- Launching your website or product within a set timeframe.
- Gaining your first 100 customers.
- Reaching a certain level of revenue within the first year.

Break down your goals into smaller, achievable **milestones** to make them feel more attainable. For instance, if your goal is to have 100 customers in six months, start by setting a goal of 10 customers within the first month.

Create a Financial Plan

Your business may need money to get off the ground and keep running. This is where your **financial plan** comes into play. You'll need to budget for the costs of starting and operating your business, including:

- **Startup costs**: These might include things like inventory, website development, legal fees, and marketing.
- **Operating costs**: Ongoing expenses such as rent, salaries, utilities, and supplies.
- **Revenue projections**: Estimate how much money you plan to make and when you expect to break even or become profitable.

A financial plan will help you understand how much capital you need, how to manage expenses, and how to track your cash flow. **Capital** refers to the **money** or **assets** that are needed to start and run a business. It includes the funds required to cover **startup costs** (such as equipment, inventory, and legal fees) and **operating expenses** (like rent, salaries, and utilities). Capital can come from different sources, such as personal savings, loans, investors, or business grants. Essentially, capital is the financial resource that fuels your business and allows it to operate and grow. You may need to seek **funding** if your initial capital is not enough. Consider funding options such as personal savings, loans, investors, or crowdfunding platforms.

Legal and Administrative Considerations

As you start your business, you need to address the legal aspects of running a company. This might include:

- Choosing a **business structure** (sole proprietorship, LLC, corporation, etc.).
- Registering your business with the appropriate government authorities.
- Getting the necessary **licenses and permits** for your industry.
- Setting up a business **bank account** and tracking your finances.
- Ensuring you have the appropriate **insurance** (business, liability, etc.).

These legal and administrative tasks may seem overwhelming, but they're essential for protecting your business and making sure everything is in compliance with the law.

Marketing and Selling: Turning Your Idea Into Revenue

Once you have a solid business plan and a product or service that solves a problem, the next step is **marketing** and **selling**. These are the processes that help you reach your target audience, communicate the value of your product or service, and ultimately convert leads into paying customers. Understanding how to effectively market and sell your product is crucial to your business's success. Let's explore both marketing and selling in detail.

Marketing: Building Awareness and Interest

Marketing is all about **creating awareness** and **generating interest** in your business. It's how you let potential customers know that your product or service exists and why it's worth their time and money. Effective marketing focuses on reaching the right people with the right message, in the right place, and at the right time.

Identifying Your Target Audience

Before you start marketing your product, you must first define who your **target audience** is. These are the people who are most likely to benefit from your product or service. Understanding their demographics, interests, and needs will help you tailor your marketing efforts to speak directly to them.

For example, if you're selling fitness equipment, your target audience might be people who are interested in health, exercise, and wellness. You need to consider factors like age, location, income level, and buying habits. The better you understand your audience, the more effectively you can reach them.

The Importance of Branding: Beyond Aesthetics

When most people think of **branding**, they think of logos, colors, and designs. While these elements are an important part of the visual identity of your business, **branding** goes much deeper than just aesthetics. At its core, branding is about the **emotional connection** your customers have with your business, how they perceive you, and the overall experience they have when interacting with your products or services.

A strong brand is more than just a logo or a catchy slogan—it's the **story** of your business, the **values** you stand for, and how you make people feel. It's the way your business communicates with customers, how you solve their problems, and the trust you build over time. Effective branding helps differentiate your business from competitors, builds loyalty, and drives long-term success.

Branding helps to differentiate your business from competitors and build trust with potential customers. It's important that your brand identity reflects the value you offer and resonates with your target audience. Consistency is key—whether someone is visiting your website, following you on social media, or seeing an advertisement, the messaging and visual elements should be aligned and professional.

Branding is about creating an emotional connection with your customers and communicating the values and personality of your business. It's the way customers feel when they interact with your business, and it plays a crucial role in building trust, standing out in the market, and fostering loyalty.

When it comes to **building trust and credibility**, your brand image helps establish whether people will choose to engage with your business. A consistent and professional brand makes your business look reliable and trustworthy, which increases the likelihood that customers will make a purchase or recommend you to others.

Creating an **emotional connection** with your audience is another essential part of branding. When people feel connected to a brand, they are more likely to become loyal customers. This emotional bond can stem from a company's story, values, or how the product or service makes people feel.

Branding also helps with **differentiation in the market**, allowing your business to stand out, even when products and services seem similar. A strong brand communicates clearly what your business stands for and how it is different from competitors.

Beyond creating awareness, a strong brand also helps build **loyalty and retention**. When customers have positive experiences with your brand—whether it's through your product, customer service, or values—they are more likely to return. This loyalty can lead to long-term relationships, turning your customers into advocates for your brand.

Consistency across all touchpoints is crucial for building a recognizable and reliable brand. Whether it's your website, social media, or customer interactions, ensuring a consistent message and tone helps establish trust with your audience. When your branding is unified, it reinforces the image you want to portray and helps your customers feel confident in your business.

Branding can significantly impact pricing and perceived value. A strong brand allows you to charge a premium for your product or service because customers associate your brand with higher quality, reliability, or status.

Choosing Your Marketing Channels

Once you've identified your audience and built your brand, you need to choose how to communicate with your audience. This involves selecting the right marketing channels to reach your customers effectively. There are many channels to consider, depending on your product and audience:

- **Social Media**: Platforms like Facebook, Instagram, TikTok, and LinkedIn are great for building brand awareness, engaging with customers, and running targeted ads.
- **Email Marketing**: Sending regular emails to subscribers can help keep your business top-of-mind, offer promotions, or share valuable content that aligns with your audience's interests.
- **Content Marketing**: Creating valuable content, such as blog posts, videos, or podcasts, helps attract potential customers by offering useful information or entertainment.
- **Search Engine Optimization (SEO)**: Optimizing your website for search engines like Google helps your business show up when people search for related products or services.
- **Paid Advertising**: Using platforms like Google Ads or Facebook Ads to promote your business to a targeted audience can help you drive more traffic and conversions, though it often requires a budget.

Crafting a Compelling Message

Your marketing message should focus on the benefits of your product or service, rather than just the features. Customers want to know how your product will solve their problems or improve their lives. A strong marketing message is clear, concise, and communicates the value you offer.

For example, instead of just saying, "Our blender has 10 speeds," you might say, "Our blender helps you make smoothies in seconds, so you can start your day with healthy energy." The second message speaks directly to the consumer's desire for health and convenience.

Tracking and Measuring Results

Effective marketing requires you to track your efforts to see what's working and what isn't. **Analytics tools** allow you to measure website traffic, social media engagement, email open rates, and conversion rates. Regularly reviewing these metrics will help you understand which strategies are generating results and where you may need to adjust your approach.

Develop a Marketing Strategy

Once your business is ready, you need a strategy to attract and retain customers. A **marketing plan** outlines how you will promote your business and generate sales. Consider:

- **Targeting the right audience**: Who are your ideal customers, and how can you reach them?
- **Branding**: What will your business stand for, and how will you present yourself to the market? This includes designing a logo, creating a brand identity, and determining your voice and messaging.
- **Marketing channels**: How will you get the word out? Social media, online advertising, email marketing, and content marketing are all effective ways to build awareness and generate leads.

A well-executed marketing strategy will help your business grow and build lasting customer relationships.

Prepare for Scaling

As your business grows, you'll want to plan for **scaling**—the process of increasing your capacity to serve more customers or expand into new markets. This might involve:

- Hiring additional staff or outsourcing tasks.
- Expanding your product line or service offerings.
- Increasing your marketing efforts to reach new customers.
- Exploring new locations or online platforms.

Planning for scaling from the start helps ensure that your business can handle growth when the time comes, without losing quality or customer satisfaction.

A well-thought-out business plan is crucial for the success of any startup. It provides clarity, direction, and helps you navigate the challenges of entrepreneurship. By carefully defining your business idea, researching the market, setting clear goals, and managing your finances, you set a solid foundation for long-term success. Planning your business not only increases your chances of success, but it also boosts your confidence by giving you a roadmap to follow as you work toward your goals.

The Art of Selling: Turning Interest into Profit

Selling is a critical part of growing your business, and it goes beyond simply having a product or service people want to buy. It's about understanding your customer's needs, building a relationship, addressing concerns, and guiding them through the buying process. Successful selling is about creating a positive experience for your customers, making them feel valued, and ultimately, earning their trust.

While marketing brings people to your business, **selling** turns them into paying customers. It's the step where you make the case for why your product or service is the solution they've been looking for and why it's worth their investment.

Building Relationships and Trust

Successful selling is not just transactional—it's about building lasting relationships with your customers. **Trust** plays a key role here. When customers trust you, they are more likely to buy from you and even return for future purchases. Building trust starts with being transparent, honest, and reliable in your interactions.

Engage with your customers by listening to their concerns and needs, and showing empathy. Instead of rushing to make a sale, take the time to get to know the customer, understand their challenges, and offer solutions. This can be as simple as asking the right questions, making sure you fully understand their requirements before offering a solution. By doing this, you create an environment where customers feel comfortable buying from you, knowing that you have their best interest in mind.

A key part of this relationship-building is **active listening**. Let your customers feel heard and understood. When a customer feels like you're genuinely trying to solve their problem, they're much more likely to make a purchase.

Identifying Needs and Offering the Right Solution

Effective selling is about understanding why a customer wants your product or service. Every customer is looking for a solution to a specific problem. Your job is to understand that need and position your product or service as the solution.

For example, if a customer is looking for a new pair of running shoes, they may be concerned with comfort, durability, or performance. A successful salesperson would not simply sell them any pair of shoes; instead, they would ask questions to understand the customer's specific needs—like their running habits or foot issues—and suggest shoes that meet those specific needs. By offering the right solution, you demonstrate that your product is valuable and that you understand the customer's problem.

Sometimes, customers may not even fully know what they need or why they are looking for a particular solution. This is where effective questioning can come into play. By asking the right questions, you guide them through the process of identifying their own needs.

Overcoming Objections

Every salesperson faces objections. An objection is any reason a potential customer has for hesitating or not committing to a purchase. Whether it's a concern about price, the product's features, or the competition, handling objections effectively is an essential part of selling.

The key to handling objections is not to get defensive or argue with the customer. Instead, approach objections as opportunities to **address concerns** and provide additional information. Listen to the objection carefully and respond thoughtfully. For example, if a customer says your product is too expensive, you could explain the value it offers, the durability of the product, or any guarantees that make it a better investment in the long run.

Another approach is to **reframe the objection**. If a customer hesitates because they're unsure of the product's benefits, reframe their concern by highlighting features that align with their needs. If price is an issue, you might offer payment plans or a discount to make the product more accessible.

It's important to remember that objections are natural. People want to be sure they are making a wise decision, so they will often express concerns. Responding to objections with understanding and solutions helps build trust and leads to more successful sales.

Creating a Sense of Urgency

Sometimes, customers need a little push to make a decision. **Creating a sense of urgency** can be a helpful tool, as long as it's done ethically. Urgency encourages customers to take action quickly rather than putting off their decision, which might cause them to forget or lose interest.

One way to create urgency is by offering **limited-time discounts** or

exclusive deals. For example, you might offer a "flash sale" or a special promotion that expires soon, encouraging the customer to act now. Another way is to highlight the **limited availability** of your product, especially if you're selling a popular or seasonal item.

It's important to strike the right balance. The urgency should feel natural, not forced. You want the customer to feel like they are making a timely decision, not like they're being rushed into something they don't want.

Closing the Sale

Closing the sale is the final step in the sales process, and it's where you ask the customer to commit to a purchase. There are several strategies you can use to close the sale, but the key is to be confident, direct, and considerate of the customer's readiness to buy.

The **direct close** is simply asking if they're ready to make a purchase. For example, you might say, "Are you ready to go ahead with this order?" or "Shall I process your payment today?"

The **assumptive close** is when you proceed as though the customer has already decided to purchase, making the next step seem natural. For example, "I'll just get this wrapped up for you," or "Let me get your information to finalize the purchase."

The **urgency close**, as mentioned earlier, highlights the time-sensitive nature of the offer. This could be, "This deal ends tonight," or "There's only one item left in stock."

After closing the sale, always thank the customer and reassure them that they made the right decision. This not only reinforces their purchase but also leaves a positive impression, making it more likely that they will return in the future.

Following Up and Building Long-Term Relationships

The sales process doesn't end when a purchase is made. Following up with customers after the sale is essential for building long-term relationships and encouraging repeat business. A simple follow-up message, whether it's through email, a phone call, or even a handwritten note, shows the customer that you care about their satisfaction and value their business.

You can also use follow-up opportunities to ask for feedback, address any concerns, and introduce additional products or services they might need. A loyal customer base is one of the most valuable assets a business can have, and effective follow-up is key to creating that loyalty.

Creating a System for Your Business: The Key to Efficiency and Growth

One of the most important steps in running and growing a business is **creating systems** that streamline your operations and ensure consistency. A system is essentially a structured process that you follow to complete tasks efficiently and effectively. Systems can cover various aspects of your business, from customer service and sales to inventory management and financial tracking.

Establishing systems from the start helps you avoid chaos, reduce errors, and ensure that your business runs smoothly, even as it grows. The right systems give you more time to focus on high-level strategy and creative aspects of your business while ensuring that day-to-day tasks are handled with consistency and precision.

Automating Routine Tasks

One of the most significant benefits of creating systems is the ability to **automate** routine and repetitive tasks. Automation can save you valuable time and reduce the chances of human error. For example, you can automate tasks such as:

- **Email marketing**: Using tools like **Mailchimp** or **Constant Contact**, you can schedule regular email newsletters, promotions, and customer follow-ups to go out automatically.
- **Billing and invoicing**: Tools like **QuickBooks** or **FreshBooks** allow you to automate invoicing and payment reminders, saving time and ensuring you don't miss any important billing tasks.
- **Social media posting**: Platforms like **Hootsuite** or **Buffer** let you schedule social media posts in advance, ensuring a consistent online presence even when you're busy with other tasks.

Automation can free up time for you to focus on strategic decisions, creative work, or customer-facing activities while ensuring that the essential tasks still get done on time.

Standardizing Processes

Standardizing processes is about creating **repeatable procedures** for everything you do in your business. This includes creating **standard operating procedures (SOPs)** for common tasks, which provide step-by-step instructions on how to complete those tasks consistently and effectively. Some examples of processes you can standardize include:

- **Order fulfillment**: From receiving an order to shipping it, you can create a system that outlines exactly how to process each order, ensuring that nothing is overlooked.
- **Customer service**: Develop a system for handling customer inquiries, complaints, or returns. By providing your team with a clear set of guidelines, you ensure that customer service is always responsive and professional.
- **Hiring and onboarding**: A standardized process for hiring new employees ensures that every candidate goes through the same steps, from job posting to interviews to final offer. An onboarding system makes sure that new hires are trained efficiently and start their jobs with

the necessary resources.

By documenting and following these processes, you ensure that your business operates efficiently and that your team is aligned in how they approach everyday tasks. This consistency also ensures that customers receive the same high level of service every time they interact with your business.

Organizing Your Financial Management

Financial systems are the backbone of your business's health. Having clear and effective systems in place for managing your finances is essential to track your revenue, expenses, and cash flow. Without a proper financial system, you may end up with inaccurate records, missed payments, or unexpected financial issues.

Some key financial systems to set up include:

- **Tracking expenses and income**: Use accounting software like **Quick-Books** or **Xero** to track your income and expenses, generate financial reports, and keep your business's finances in order. These tools can also help you with tax preparation and ensuring you meet regulatory requirements.
- **Budgeting**: Establishing a budgeting system will help you plan for future expenses and set aside money for key areas like marketing, expansion, or hiring new employees.
- **Financial forecasting**: Regularly forecasting your business's financial performance allows you to predict future cash flow and make data-driven decisions on how to allocate resources or adjust pricing.

Having a solid financial system in place not only ensures you stay organized but also helps you make informed decisions and secure funding when needed.

Managing Customer Relationships

An effective **Customer Relationship Management (CRM) system** helps you manage interactions with customers and prospects, track sales, and build long-lasting relationships. CRM systems like **Salesforce**, **HubSpot**, or **Zoho CRM** can help automate customer follow-ups, manage your sales pipeline, and ensure that your team is always on top of customer needs.

Here's how a CRM system can help:

- **Track customer interactions**: You can log customer interactions, emails, phone calls, and meetings in one place, allowing you to understand your customer's journey and preferences.
- **Segment your audience**: With a CRM, you can segment your customers by demographics, interests, purchase history, or engagement level, enabling you to send targeted marketing campaigns and personalized messages.
- **Improve customer service**: By keeping a history of customer issues, queries, and complaints, your team can respond more quickly and effectively, improving the overall customer experience.

An efficient CRM system can enhance customer satisfaction, streamline your sales efforts, and make your marketing campaigns more targeted and effective.

Inventory and Supply Chain Management

If you sell physical products, it's essential to have an organized system in place for **inventory management**. Without it, you risk running out of stock, overstocking, or losing track of products, which can lead to frustrated customers and lost revenue.

Using inventory management tools like **TradeGecko**, **Odoo**, or **Cin7** helps you track stock levels, manage suppliers, and automate reorder processes. These systems can alert you when inventory is running low, so you can reorder in time and avoid stockouts. They also help streamline supply chain management, which ensures that products are delivered on time and costs are kept under control.

An efficient inventory system will help you avoid waste, manage production schedules, and provide better service to your customers by ensuring that you have the right products available when they need them.

Monitoring and Improving Performance

To ensure your business is running smoothly, it's crucial to monitor your **business performance** regularly. This means tracking key metrics like:

- **Sales performance**: Are your sales growing or declining? Are you meeting your targets?
- **Customer satisfaction**: Are customers happy with your product or service? What feedback are they giving?
- **Operational efficiency**: Are your processes running smoothly? Are there any bottlenecks or inefficiencies?

Using data to monitor your performance allows you to identify areas for improvement. If a certain system isn't working as expected, you can make adjustments quickly to ensure that your business continues to move forward.

Additionally, continually refining your systems as you learn more about your business will help you stay competitive, adapt to changing markets, and scale your operations more effectively.

Preparing for Growth

As your business grows, your systems need to be scalable. This means building processes that can handle increased demand without compromising quality or efficiency. For instance:

- **Expanding your team**: You may need to onboard new employees, which means creating scalable hiring and training systems.

- **Automating more processes**: As you grow, look for additional areas of your business where automation can save time or reduce errors.
- **Scaling operations**: You may need to invest in more inventory, additional locations, or upgraded technology to handle the increased volume of customers or orders.

Having systems in place that are adaptable and scalable will ensure that your business can grow without becoming overwhelmed. This allows you to manage new challenges effectively and continue to deliver value to your customers.

The Power of Systems in Business

Creating and maintaining effective systems is one of the most important things you can do for your business. Systems help ensure that your business runs efficiently, your customers are happy, and you're able to scale and adapt as your business grows. By automating tasks, standardizing processes, organizing finances, and managing customer relationships, you create a strong foundation that will support the long-term success and sustainability of your business. With the right systems in place, you can focus more on growing your business and less on managing day-to-day operations.

Chapter 9

Understanding Taxes: Why We Pay and How It Works

"Money is a tool. Used properly, it makes something beautiful; used wrongly, it makes a mess!" — Bradley Vinson

Taxes are an essential part of the financial system, but they can often feel confusing or overwhelming, especially for new business owners or individuals who are just starting to get a handle on their finances. Understanding taxes is crucial because they play a significant role in how much of your income or profits you get to keep and how much you owe to the government. In this section, we'll break down the basics of taxes, explain why we pay them, and help you understand how they work in the context of both personal finances and business.

Why Do We Pay Taxes?

Taxes are how governments fund the services and infrastructure that we rely on every day. From public schools, roads, and hospitals to law enforcement, social security, and defense, taxes are the primary way that the government raises money to support these services. Without taxes, governments wouldn't be able to provide the services that benefit society as a whole.

When you pay taxes, you are contributing to the common good. Everyone pays taxes—whether through income tax, sales tax, property tax, or other types—depending on the laws of the country and state in which they live. The amount you pay is generally based on how much you earn, how much property you own, or how much you spend, though the specifics can vary widely.

How Do Taxes Work?

At its core, **taxation** is the process through which individuals and businesses contribute a portion of their income or profits to the government. There are several types of taxes that people and businesses are required to pay:

1. **Income Tax**: This is a tax on the money you earn. For individuals, it's typically based on your salary, wages, or other sources of income (like investments or freelance work). The government taxes your income at different rates depending on how much you earn—this is often called a **progressive tax system**. The more you earn, the higher your tax rate. Business owners also pay income tax on the profits their business generates.
2. **Sales Tax**: This is a tax on goods and services you buy. For example, when you purchase an item at a store, a percentage of the sale price goes to the government as sales tax. The rate of sales tax can vary by state and even by city, and some products, like food or prescription medication, may be exempt from sales tax.
3. **Property Tax**: If you own property, such as a home or business, you are likely required to pay property taxes. These taxes are typically calculated based on the value of the property. Property taxes are used to fund local government services like schools, emergency services, and infrastructure.
4. **Self-Employment Tax**: If you run a business or work as a freelancer, you may need to pay self-employment taxes. In the United States, for example, self-employed individuals are responsible for paying both the employee and employer portions of Social Security and Medicare taxes.

This tax is in addition to your regular income tax.

5. **Corporate Taxes**: For business owners, there is also **corporate tax**. Businesses are taxed on their profits, and the tax rate depends on the structure of the business (e.g., LLC, corporation, sole proprietorship). Corporations typically pay a fixed percentage of their profits in taxes.

6. **Other Taxes**: There are various other taxes that may apply, such as **estate taxes**, **capital gains taxes** (on profits made from the sale of assets like property or stocks), **excise taxes** (on specific goods like gasoline), and **import/export duties** (on goods being traded internationally).

How Taxes Are Calculated

The way your taxes are calculated depends on several factors, including the type of tax, your income level, and any deductions or credits you may qualify for. Let's break down how this works for a few key taxes:

- **Income Tax**: Income tax is typically calculated based on **tax brackets**, which divide income into ranges that are taxed at different rates. For example, you might pay 10% on the first $10,000 of your income, 20% on the next $30,000, and 30% on any income above that. This structure means that your overall tax rate depends on your total income. Most tax systems allow for **tax deductions** (e.g., for student loan interest or business expenses) that can reduce the amount of taxable income, and **tax credits** (e.g., for education or dependent children) that directly reduce the amount of tax you owe.

- **Sales Tax**: Sales tax is calculated as a percentage of the sale price of the product or service. If the sales tax rate is 8%, and you buy an item for $50, the sales tax would be $4, making the total cost $54. Sales tax is typically collected by the seller at the time of purchase and then paid to the government.

- **Property Tax**: Property taxes are calculated based on the value of the property you own. For example, if your home is valued at $200,000 and your local property tax rate is 2%, your property tax bill would be $4,000 for the year.

How Taxes Impact Your Business

If you own a business, taxes can become more complex. **Business taxes** vary depending on the structure of your business (sole proprietorship, LLC, corporation, etc.), the type of business you run, and where you're located. Here are some key points for business owners to keep in mind:

1. **Business Income Taxes**: Your business's profits are typically subject to income tax. This means that after you subtract your business expenses (such as rent, wages, and supplies), the remaining profit is taxed. The amount of tax you owe depends on your business structure, the amount of profit you make, and local tax rates.
2. **Sales Tax**: If your business sells products or services, you may be required to collect **sales tax** from your customers and remit it to the government. This can involve regular reporting and keeping track of sales in different states or countries, as sales tax rates can vary widely.
3. **Payroll Taxes**: If you have employees, you are responsible for withholding **income tax** from their wages and paying the employer's portion of social security, Medicare, and unemployment taxes. You'll also need to report and pay these taxes regularly to the appropriate government agencies.
4. **Business Deductions**: Many business expenses can be deducted from your taxable income, such as office supplies, employee salaries, marketing costs, and other operating expenses. Keeping detailed records of these expenses is critical to ensuring you pay the correct amount of tax and maximize your deductions.

Tax Filing and Deadlines

Understanding **tax filing** deadlines is crucial to avoid penalties. For individuals, tax returns are typically due on **April 15th** each year, though deadlines may vary depending on the country. For businesses, tax deadlines depend on the business structure and the type of taxes being filed. You'll need to file an **annual tax return** with the appropriate tax authority (e.g., the IRS in the U.S.), and some taxes, such as payroll or sales tax, may require more frequent filings.

Tax Planning and Seeking Help

Tax planning involves organizing your financial affairs in a way that minimizes your tax burden. This can involve taking advantage of tax **deductions**, **credits**, and other strategies. Some common tax planning tactics include contributing to retirement accounts, claiming business expenses, and using tax credits for things like education or dependents.

Many people and businesses benefit from seeking help from a **tax professional** or **accountant** who can offer guidance and ensure that taxes are filed correctly. Tax professionals are especially helpful for individuals with more complicated tax situations (like self-employed individuals or business owners) and can help you maximize your deductions and credits.

The Importance of Good Record Keeping for Taxes

Good record keeping is crucial for both **personal and business finances**, especially when it comes to taxes. Keeping organized and detailed records helps you stay compliant with tax laws and can save you time and money during tax season. Proper documentation ensures that you can claim all eligible deductions, report your income accurately, and avoid penalties for missing or incorrect information.

For businesses, keeping track of **receipts**, **invoices**, **bank statements**, **payroll records**, and **expense reports** is essential. This allows you to accurately calculate your profits, claim deductions, and ensure that your tax filings are correct. For individuals, keeping records of things like **medical expenses**, **donations**, and **business-related expenses** can help you reduce your taxable income and maximize potential refunds or tax credits.

Investing time in creating a reliable record-keeping system—whether it's through digital tools, accounting software, or simple manual methods—can provide peace of mind, prevent costly mistakes, and make tax time much easier to navigate. Proper record keeping isn't just for tax filings; it's a crucial part of maintaining the financial health of your business and personal finances year-round.

Taxes are an inevitable part of life, but understanding how they work can empower you to make better financial decisions. Whether you're filing taxes for yourself or managing a business, knowing what types of taxes apply to you and how they're calculated will help you stay compliant and avoid unnecessary costs. With proper planning and the right support, you can manage your tax obligations in a way that minimizes stress and maximizes your financial success.

Chapter 10

Understanding Insurance: Protecting Your Future and Finances

"Success depends upon previous preparation, and without such preparation there is sure to be failure." - Confucius

Insurance is one of the most important tools for protecting yourself, your family, and your business from financial risks. While it may feel like an added cost, insurance provides a safety net, helping you recover financially from unexpected events such as accidents, illness, property damage, or loss of income.

What is Insurance?

In simple terms, **insurance** is a contract between you and an insurance company where you pay regular premiums in exchange for financial protection against specific risks. If something covered by the insurance happens (like an accident, illness, or damage), the insurance company helps cover the costs. The amount you pay for insurance is known as the **premium**, and the amount the insurance company will pay in case of a claim is known as the **coverage** or **benefit**.

There are different types of insurance designed to protect you in different areas of life. Some common types include:

- **Health Insurance**: Covers medical expenses like doctor visits, hospital stays, and prescriptions.
- **Life Insurance**: Provides financial support to your beneficiaries if you pass away.
- **Auto Insurance**: Covers damage to your car or injuries sustained in an accident.
- **Homeowners or Renters Insurance**: Protects your home and belongings from damage or theft.
- **Disability Insurance**: Replaces a portion of your income if you are unable to work due to illness or injury.
- **Business Insurance**: Protects your business against risks like property damage, liability claims, or loss of income.

While insurance helps protect you financially, it also has an impact on your overall finances. Understanding how insurance works and selecting the right coverage for your needs is critical to managing your personal and business financial health.

How Insurance Affects Your Finances

While insurance is an ongoing expense, it has the potential to save you much more in case of a large unexpected event. Here's how insurance can affect your finances:

1. **Financial Protection and Peace of Mind** Insurance gives you the **peace of mind** that if something unexpected happens, you won't face the financial burden alone. For example, without health insurance, a major illness or accident could result in medical bills that you might struggle to pay. But with insurance, those costs are covered, and you won't need to dip into savings or take on debt.
2. Similarly, **life insurance** ensures that your loved ones will have financial

support in the event of your passing. This can help cover funeral expenses, mortgage payments, and other costs, preventing your family from facing a financial crisis during an already difficult time.

3. **Managing Risk** Insurance allows you to **transfer risk** to the insurance company. Instead of carrying the full burden of a potential financial loss (e.g., damage to your car, house, or business), you share that risk with your insurer. For example, in the case of auto insurance, if your car is damaged in an accident, the insurance company will cover the repair costs, which could otherwise be an overwhelming financial burden.

4. For businesses, insurance is even more critical. Without the right insurance, a single lawsuit or unexpected incident (like a fire or theft) could result in bankruptcy. Having the appropriate business insurance allows your company to continue operating smoothly, even in the face of significant financial challenges.

5. **Cost of Premiums** The biggest immediate impact of insurance on your finances is the **cost of premiums**. Premiums are paid regularly—monthly, quarterly, or annually—and can add up over time. For some individuals and businesses, these premiums can be a significant part of their budget.

6. However, it's important to remember that the cost of insurance is a trade-off for the financial protection it provides. Without insurance, you could face far higher costs if something goes wrong. For instance, paying for health insurance might feel like a burden, but if you become seriously ill, it could save you thousands of dollars in medical expenses.

7. One way to reduce premium costs is by carefully reviewing the **deductibles** and **coverage limits**. A higher deductible usually means a lower premium, but you'll need to pay more out of pocket before the insurance coverage kicks in. Choosing the right balance between premium cost and deductible is key to making insurance affordable while ensuring you're adequately protected.

8. **Building Wealth with Insurance** Some types of insurance, like **life insurance** or **whole life insurance**, can be used as a tool for **building wealth**. These types of policies build a cash value over time that can

be borrowed against or used for other financial goals. However, it's important to weigh the pros and cons of these policies because they tend to have higher premiums than other types of life insurance, like term life insurance.

9. Additionally, insurance can play a key role in **protecting your business assets**, which, in turn, contributes to long-term financial success. For example, **business interruption insurance** helps ensure that your business can survive and recover financially if a disaster or event forces you to temporarily shut down. This protection gives you the security to make long-term investments in your business without the risk of a sudden financial crisis taking it all away.

10. **Risk of Underinsurance** While having insurance is important, **underinsurance** can have a negative impact on your finances. Underinsurance means having insufficient coverage to meet your needs. For instance, if your home is underinsured and suffers significant damage, the insurance company may not cover all of the costs, leaving you to cover the gap.

11. For individuals, this can mean facing out-of-pocket expenses for medical bills, property repairs, or lost income. For businesses, underinsurance can lead to financial ruin, as the company may not be able to recover from a significant financial loss.

12. Regularly reviewing your coverage and adjusting it to match your current situation is crucial to ensuring that you are properly insured. As your life or business grows, your insurance needs will evolve, and it's important to keep your coverage up-to-date.

13. **Tax Implications of Insurance** Some types of insurance, like **health insurance** or **business insurance**, may have **tax benefits**. For example, many countries allow you to deduct the cost of health insurance premiums from your taxable income, lowering your overall tax burden. For businesses, premiums for certain types of insurance, like liability or property insurance, can be tax-deductible as a business expense.

14. On the other hand, some life insurance policies may not have immediate tax benefits, but the death benefit paid out to beneficiaries is often **tax-free**. Understanding the tax implications of different types of insurance

can help you make the most of your financial planning.

Choosing the Right Insurance for Your Needs

Choosing the right type and amount of insurance depends on your individual or business needs, risk tolerance, and financial situation. Here are a few general guidelines:

- **For individuals**, start by getting the basics covered, like health insurance, life insurance, and auto insurance. Then, consider other types based on your needs, such as renters or homeowners insurance.
- **For businesses**, consider essential coverage such as liability insurance, property insurance, and workers' compensation. As your business grows, you may also want to explore additional coverage like business interruption or professional liability insurance.

Consulting with an insurance advisor or financial planner can help ensure that you select the right policies for your situation and that you aren't over- or under-insured.

Protecting Your Financial Future

Insurance plays a key role in protecting your finances from unexpected events. While paying for insurance premiums may feel like an additional expense, the protection and peace of mind it provides are invaluable. By understanding how different types of insurance work and choosing the right coverage, you can ensure that both you and your business are safeguarded from financial hardship. In the long run, insurance is not just an expense—it's an investment in your financial security and future.

Chapter 11

The Art of Negotiation: Getting What You Want

"Successful negotiation is not about getting to 'yes'; it's about mastering 'no' and understanding what the path to an agreement is." – Christopher Voss

Negotiation is a skill that many people think only experts or business people need to master, but in reality, **negotiation** is something we all use every day. Whether you're buying a car, asking for a raise, or even discussing household responsibilities, negotiating is an essential part of getting what you want and need from different situations.

Negotiation isn't about being aggressive or manipulative; it's about understanding your needs and the other person's needs, finding common ground, and reaching an agreement that benefits both sides. It's a way to communicate more effectively and achieve outcomes that leave everyone feeling satisfied. By learning how to negotiate, you can improve your finances, boost your career, and create better relationships—both personally and professionally.

What is Negotiation?

At its core, **negotiation** is a conversation where two or more parties with different needs or perspectives come together to find a mutually acceptable solution. You can negotiate over nearly anything: salaries, prices, terms of service, or even daily chores at home.

For example, if you're buying a car, the dealer may have a set price, but through negotiation, you can often get a better deal. Similarly, when negotiating a salary, you can often convince your employer to offer a higher wage or additional benefits based on the value you bring to the company.

Negotiation is about reaching a deal where both sides feel they've won something, and both parties leave the conversation feeling like their needs were heard and respected.

The Basics of Negotiation

The first step in any negotiation is **preparation**. Before you sit down to negotiate, take the time to:

- **Understand your needs**: What do you want to get out of the situation? Be clear about your goals and what you're willing to compromise on. This could be a price, a deadline, or a benefit.
- **Know the other party's needs**: Try to understand what the other person wants out of the negotiation. Are they looking to close a sale, or are they trying to keep costs down? Knowing their goals can help you figure out how to make the negotiation work for both sides.
- **Set your limits**: Know your **bottom line**—the point at which you're willing to walk away. If you're buying a product, for example, figure out the maximum price you're willing to pay before you start negotiating.

Once you have this information, you can begin the negotiation with confidence, knowing exactly where you stand and what you're aiming for.

Active Listening and Communication

Active listening is one of the most important skills in negotiation. You can't get what you want if you don't first understand the needs and concerns of the other party. When negotiating, listen carefully to what the other person is saying, ask open-ended questions, and try to identify their interests.

For example, if you're negotiating a pay raise, instead of simply stating that you want more money, try asking your boss about the company's goals for the year and how you can align your work to meet those goals. This shows that you are not only interested in your own needs but are also thinking about the bigger picture.

Active listening also involves **reading between the lines**. Pay attention to the tone of the conversation and any non-verbal cues (body language or facial expressions), which can provide additional insight into what the other party is really thinking.

Finding Common Ground

Negotiation is not about winning or losing—it's about finding a **mutually beneficial solution**. Think of it as a problem-solving process. The best negotiations are those where both sides feel like they've gained something valuable. This means that instead of only focusing on your own needs, you should also be looking for ways to give the other party something they want or need.

For example, if you're negotiating a salary, while your goal might be to earn more, the employer might be concerned about staying within budget. You could offer to take on more responsibilities or help with a project, demonstrating the value you bring. In return, they might be more willing to meet your salary expectations.

Finding common ground requires flexibility and creativity. Often, there is more than one way to reach an agreement. By keeping the conversation open and collaborative, you increase your chances of coming to a favorable outcome for everyone involved.

Be Confident But Respectful

Confidence is key in negotiation. When you're clear about your needs and prepared with facts or reasoning, you're more likely to be taken seriously. Don't be afraid to express your expectations, but remember, being **respectful** is just as important as being confident.

Using phrases like, "I believe my experience warrants this increase" or "I've done some research and found that the typical salary range for this role is...," shows that you've done your homework and are confident in your position. However, be careful not to come across as rude or demanding—negotiation is a **conversation**, not a confrontation.

Confidence also means being **comfortable with silence**. Sometimes, the other party might need time to think about your offer. Don't rush to fill the silence with pressure; instead, let them consider your proposal and respond when they are ready.

Negotiation Tactics and Strategies

There are several tactics you can use to improve your chances of getting a favorable deal:

- **Anchoring**: This is when you start with an offer that's more favorable to you than what you actually expect to get. For example, if you're buying a used car, you might start with a low offer to leave room for negotiation. The idea is that the other party will adjust their expectations based on your starting point.
- **BATNA (Best Alternative to a Negotiated Agreement)**: Know your alternatives. If you're negotiating a job offer, for example, you may want to know what other opportunities are available to you. If you don't reach a deal, you should have a clear idea of what your options are.
- **Reciprocity**: When the other party makes a concession (like offering you a discount), be sure to offer something in return. This could be a small compromise on your side, showing that you're willing to meet them

halfway.

- **The "Silent Pause"**: Sometimes, the best way to push the other party to make a concession is by staying silent after making an offer or statement. The pause creates pressure on the other side to respond.

Handling Rejection and Compromise

Not every negotiation will go as planned. Sometimes, your first offer will be rejected, or the other party may not agree to the terms you wanted. This is where your ability to handle rejection and compromise comes into play. Stay calm and **remain flexible**.

If your offer is rejected, don't take it personally. Instead, ask the other person why they said no and see if there is a way to adjust your proposal to meet their needs. It's important to be willing to **negotiate again**—sometimes, the first offer isn't the final one.

Also, be prepared to **compromise**. In many cases, you may not get everything you want, but by being open to adjusting your expectations, you can still find a solution that works for both sides.

Focus on Interests, Not Positions

Often, negotiations break down when both parties focus solely on their positions—what they **want**—rather than the underlying interests—why they want it. To negotiate successfully, try to understand the **interests** behind the other party's position. This will allow you to find creative solutions that satisfy both sides.

For example, if you're negotiating a contract with a supplier and they are hesitant to lower their price due to their own cost structure, their interest might be in maintaining profitability. Instead of focusing solely on getting a discount, you could offer solutions such as committing to larger, more frequent orders or offering to pay early to improve their cash flow. By aligning your needs with their goals, you create a win-win situation that strengthens the relationship while addressing both parties' interests.

Keep Your Emotions in Check

Negotiation can sometimes be emotional, especially when it involves something important to you—whether it's money, a job offer, or personal matters. However, letting emotions drive your decisions can make it harder to think clearly and could jeopardize the negotiation. Staying calm, composed, and professional will help you stay in control of the situation.

If you feel yourself getting upset or frustrated, it's okay to take a break and come back to the conversation when you've regained your composure. This also gives the other party a chance to cool down if the discussion is becoming too heated.

Know When to Walk Away

One of the most powerful negotiation tactics is the ability to walk away if the terms aren't favorable to you. Knowing when to **walk away** gives you leverage because it signals that you're not desperate for a deal. Having a clear understanding of your **BATNA** (Best Alternative to a Negotiated Agreement) is critical—this is your best option if the negotiation falls through. If the offer isn't meeting your needs or expectations, walking away can often lead the other party to make a better offer.

It's important to approach this with confidence, not arrogance. When you walk away, do so respectfully and leave the door open for future discussions, but don't settle for terms that don't align with your needs.

Use Timing to Your Advantage

Timing can play a crucial role in successful negotiations. Be mindful of when you choose to make an offer or propose a deal. Sometimes, timing can help you get more favorable terms. Here are a few timing-related tips:

- **Choose the right moment**: If you're negotiating a raise, for example, pick a time when your boss is in a good mood or after you've completed

130

a major project successfully.

- **Delay your response**: If you're presented with an offer, take your time before giving an answer. A pause or delay can create the impression that you're carefully considering the proposal and may lead the other side to offer a better deal.
- **Close on a high note**: Timing can also be used when wrapping up a negotiation. The last thing you say is often what sticks with the other party, so make sure it's a positive note that reinforces your satisfaction with the agreement.

Practice Reciprocity

Reciprocity is the principle that when one side gives something, the other side feels compelled to give something in return. You can use this principle to your advantage during a negotiation. When the other party makes a concession, offer something in return. This can be as simple as agreeing to a small point in their favor or offering a compromise.

For example, if a seller offers you a discount, you might reciprocate by agreeing to buy a larger quantity or paying immediately. This mutual give-and-take shows that both sides are working together, building goodwill, and making the negotiation feel more collaborative.

Be Prepared to Make the First Offer

Making the first offer in a negotiation can be intimidating, but studies show that people who make the first offer often end up with more favorable results. When you make the first offer, you set the **anchor point**, which influences the rest of the conversation. For example, if you're negotiating a salary, starting with a higher figure gives you room to come down while still staying within your target range.

However, this strategy only works if you've done your research and know the value of what you're negotiating for. Making an informed first offer shows confidence and positions you as someone who understands what's fair.

Maintain a Positive Attitude

A positive attitude goes a long way in negotiations. Being respectful, optimistic, and open to dialogue can foster a cooperative atmosphere that encourages both sides to work towards a solution. If the negotiation is tense, try to remain calm and positive—it shows maturity and professionalism, which can lead to better outcomes.

Additionally, using **positive language** can make the negotiation process smoother. For example, instead of saying, "I can't accept that offer," say, "I would feel more comfortable if we could adjust the offer in this way…" This shifts the conversation toward collaboration rather than confrontation.

Know Your Worth

Understanding your **value** is one of the most important factors in any negotiation. Whether you're negotiating a salary, a contract, or the price of a product, knowing what you bring to the table and being confident in your worth will give you the leverage you need to secure a good deal.

If you're negotiating a raise, for example, be prepared to back up your request with examples of your achievements, your contributions, and the value you bring to the company. The more information and proof you have, the stronger your position will be.

Keep the Long-Term Relationship in Mind

Negotiation is not just about one deal—it's about building long-term relationships. Whether it's with an employer, client, or vendor, maintaining a good relationship after the negotiation is essential for future opportunities. While you may win a negotiation by getting exactly what you want, if the other party feels manipulated or unfairly treated, it can sour the relationship and hurt your reputation.

Always keep the big picture in mind. A fair, respectful negotiation creates trust and opens the door for future collaboration and mutual benefits.

Closing the Deal

Once you've found common ground and both parties have agreed to the terms, it's time to **close the deal**. Be clear about what has been agreed upon, and confirm that everyone is on the same page. This may involve signing a contract, making a payment, or simply shaking hands.

A successful negotiation ends with both sides feeling like they've gotten something valuable. Don't forget to express your appreciation for the other party's willingness to negotiate, as this fosters goodwill and leaves the door open for future negotiations.

Mastering Negotiation

The art of negotiation is a vital skill that can significantly impact your personal and professional life. It's about balancing assertiveness with cooperation, being prepared with information, and understanding the needs of both parties. Whether you're negotiating a raise, a business contract, or even the price of something you're buying, the key is to be confident, patient, and strategic. By applying these tips and strategies, you can ensure that you get what you want while maintaining positive, long-lasting relationships with others.

Chapter 12

The Power of Giving: Embracing Philanthropy and Making a Difference

"No act of kindness, no matter how small, is ever wasted." - Aesop

In a world where financial success is often measured by wealth and material possessions, it's easy to forget that the true power of money lies not in what you can acquire, but in what you can give. Embracing philanthropy is not just about charity; it's about creating a ripple effect that spreads kindness, generosity, and positive change throughout the world. **Philanthropy** is the act of **giving** or **donating** resources, such as money, time, or expertise, to support causes or help improve the well-being of others. It involves a selfless desire to make a positive impact in society, often by addressing social issues, supporting charitable organizations, or promoting the welfare of disadvantaged or underserved communities. The goal of philanthropy is not only to provide financial support but also to contribute to long-term positive change, improving lives and creating a better future for all.

Whether you have a little or a lot, there is always an opportunity to give, and doing so can enrich your life in ways you never expected.

Understanding the True Meaning of Philanthropy

Philanthropy isn't just about writing a check or donating to a cause—it's about **intentional, impactful giving** aimed at improving the lives of others. The word itself comes from the Greek term "philanthropia," meaning "love of humanity." It reflects the idea of giving not only from your wealth but also from your heart, supporting causes that align with your values and passions.

Philanthropy can take many forms. It can be:

- **Monetary donations** to organizations or causes.
- **Volunteering your time** and skills to help those in need.
- **Advocating for causes** that help improve communities or the world at large.
- **Supporting small businesses** or local entrepreneurs in underserved communities.

While financial contributions are often the first thing that comes to mind when people think about giving, it's important to remember that even small acts of kindness—like offering your time or expertise—can have an equally significant impact.

The Ripple Effect of Giving

One of the most powerful aspects of giving is the **ripple effect** it creates. When you help others, you not only make a difference in their lives, but you inspire them to help others as well. Giving doesn't just stop at the initial act—it spreads, multiplying its impact as it travels through communities and generations.

For example, think about how a small act of kindness can inspire someone to pay it forward. If you donate food to a local shelter, someone who receives that meal may feel moved to help others in return, whether through volunteering or donating in the future. Your contribution sets off a series of positive actions, creating a cycle of goodwill and compassion.

This ripple effect can extend beyond just individuals. By supporting **charitable organizations**, you help them expand their reach, allowing them to provide greater resources, assistance, and advocacy. Your donations, no matter how large or small, contribute to larger systemic changes that impact entire communities and even nations.

Giving for Personal Fulfillment and Growth

Philanthropy is not only a way to help others—it can also be a powerful tool for **personal growth**. Studies have shown that giving to others is directly linked to increased happiness, reduced stress, and a greater sense of purpose. In fact, the act of helping others triggers the release of endorphins and oxytocin in the brain, often referred to as the "happiness hormones." These chemicals boost feelings of joy and satisfaction, creating a sense of fulfillment that money and material possessions can't provide.

When you embrace a mindset of giving, it shifts your perspective from scarcity to abundance. Instead of focusing on what you lack or what you need, you start to see the world through a lens of opportunity—where there is always something to give, no matter your circumstances. Whether you're donating your time, expertise, or financial resources, giving cultivates an attitude of **gratitude**, which has been shown to improve mental well-being.

In essence, philanthropy allows you to grow as a person, nurturing qualities such as empathy, compassion, and generosity. Giving to others enriches your life, expanding your emotional and spiritual wealth, while also benefiting those you're helping.

How Giving Can Strengthen Your Finances

You might be wondering: how does giving impact your financial situation? In reality, embracing a giving mindset doesn't just make the world a better place—it can also be beneficial for your own financial health. When you give, you often receive in ways you may not expect.

For example, charitable donations can often be tax-deductible, allowing you to reduce your taxable income. Many people also find that giving leads to stronger **networking opportunities** and **business connections**. When you give back to your community, you build a reputation as someone who cares and is invested in the success of others, which can attract support for your own endeavors.

Giving can also help build wealth—not in the traditional sense, but in a broader way. By supporting others, you are creating a cycle of positive energy and good deeds that can lead to unexpected rewards. People who experience your generosity may want to give back to you, whether through personal or professional opportunities.

Moreover, philanthropy can encourage a more mindful approach to finances. When you regularly allocate a portion of your income to giving, it shifts your focus from material accumulation to creating long-term value and impact, which can lead to more fulfilling and intentional financial choices.

Ways to Get Started with Giving

If you're new to philanthropy, it can be difficult to know where to start. Here are some practical ways to begin:

- **Start Small**: You don't need to make huge donations to make a difference. Even small, regular contributions—whether it's money, time, or goods—can add up and have a meaningful impact. For example, consider donating a set percentage of your monthly income to a cause or volunteer a few hours each month at a local organization.
- **Find Your Passion**: Giving is most powerful when it aligns with your values. Think about the causes that matter most to you—whether it's helping underprivileged children, supporting mental health initiatives, or fighting climate change—and focus your giving efforts on these areas.
- **Leverage Your Skills**: You don't need to have a lot of money to make an impact. If financial contributions are difficult, consider donating your time or talents. Do you have a skill or expertise that could help others? Whether it's tutoring, offering free services, or mentoring someone, these

forms of giving are just as impactful.

- **Partner with Others**: Philanthropy doesn't have to be done alone. Consider pooling resources with friends, family, or coworkers to make a larger impact. Group donations or collective volunteering efforts can amplify the change you can create together.
- **Get Involved in Your Community**: Giving locally can have a significant impact. Look for opportunities to volunteer at shelters, food banks, or community outreach programs in your area. These organizations are often the lifeblood of a community and can benefit greatly from your support.

Embracing Giving as a Lifelong Practice

Philanthropy is not just a one-time activity—it's a mindset and a lifelong practice. When you integrate giving into your daily life, it transforms the way you see the world and the way you interact with others. Giving becomes less about charity and more about making a real difference. Over time, as your life and business grow, you'll find that giving is no longer just a way to help others—it becomes a core part of who you are and the legacy you leave behind.

Making a Difference, One Act at a Time

The power of giving is immense. Whether it's contributing to a charity, volunteering your time, or offering emotional support to someone in need, each act of giving has the potential to create ripples of positive change in the world. By embracing philanthropy, you not only help others but also enhance your own personal growth, financial health, and sense of purpose. Giving is not a burden—it's an opportunity to share the abundance you have and make the world a better place for everyone. Embrace the power of giving today and start making a difference, one act of kindness at a time.

Chapter 13

The Power of Diversifying Your Income

"Opportunities don't happen. You create them." — *Chris Grosser*

In today's fast-paced and unpredictable world, relying on a single source of income can be risky. What happens if you lose your job, experience a health emergency, or face an unexpected financial setback? Without a backup plan, these situations can quickly derail your financial stability. That's where diversifying your income comes in.

Diversifying income means creating multiple streams of revenue, so you're not dependent on just one paycheck or source of income. It's about being proactive and exploring new ways to earn, save, and invest your money, even while maintaining your day job. In this chapter, we'll show you how you can leverage your skills, assets, and time to build multiple income streams that provide financial security, increase your wealth, and open doors to new opportunities.

Whether you're looking to boost your savings, pay off debt, or build long-term wealth, having diverse sources of income can help you achieve your financial goals faster and with less risk. It's not just about working harder—it's about working smarter and finding ways to make money work for you.

In the following pages, we'll explore practical, beginner-friendly ideas for diversifying your income, from simple side hustles to smart investments that

can generate passive income. With the right strategies, you can take control
of your financial future and create a life of greater freedom and security.

Why Diversifying Your Income Matters

- **Increased Financial Security** When you depend on a single income
  source, your financial well-being is tied to one employer or opportunity.
  If something happens to that source—like a job loss, a company closing
  down, or a sudden change in industry trends—your financial security
  could be at risk. Diversifying your income helps spread that risk across
  different avenues, reducing the impact of any one income stream being
  affected. For example, if you rely only on your full-time job and
  unexpectedly lose it, your entire income disappears. But if you've also
  built a side hustle, invested in stocks or real estate, or have another
  freelance gig, you still have income coming in from other sources, giving
  you time to adjust and recover.
- **Accelerated Wealth Building** Diversification allows you to grow your
  wealth faster. With more than one income stream, you're able to earn
  more money, which can be reinvested into savings or investments. This
  can set you up for long-term wealth accumulation. For instance, while
  your primary job pays the bills, additional income from investments in
  stocks, real estate, or even a side business could be used to grow your
  savings or pay off debt more quickly. Over time, this leads to greater
  financial freedom and less dependency on your day job.
- **Flexibility and Freedom** One of the biggest benefits of diversifying
  your income is the flexibility it provides. Having multiple streams of
  income often means you're not locked into a set schedule or a single
  employer's terms. This can give you more control over how you spend
  your time, which projects you take on, and where you focus your energy.
  For example, if you have a steady income from a freelance business and
  rental income from a property, you might have the freedom to reduce
  your hours at your day job and focus more on your side hustles. This can
  also provide you with the ability to pursue passions, travel, or take time

off without worrying about missing a paycheck.

- **Protection Against Inflation** Another important reason to diversify your income is to protect yourself against the impact of inflation. As the cost of living increases, having just one source of income might not be enough to keep up with rising expenses. By diversifying your income, especially by investing in assets that can appreciate over time (such as real estate or stocks), you're positioning yourself to stay ahead of inflation and continue growing your wealth.

Types of Income Streams to Diversify

There are many ways you can diversify your income. Here are a few examples:

Active Income This is the money you earn through direct work or labor, such as a **full-time job**, **part-time job**, or **freelance work**. While active income is important, relying solely on it can limit your potential for wealth building, as you are essentially trading time for money.

Examples of active income include:

- Working for an employer
- Freelancing (writing, graphic design, consulting, etc.)
- Part-time gigs (like driving for a rideshare service)
- Hourly jobs or day labor

2. Portfolio Income Portfolio income comes from investments you've made, such as stocks, bonds, mutual funds, or exchange-traded funds (ETFs). With portfolio income, you earn money through dividends, interest payments, or capital gains, without actively working for it. This form of income can be more passive but requires an initial investment of time, money, and research to understand and manage.

Examples of portfolio income include:

- Dividend payments from stocks
- Interest earned on savings accounts or bonds

- Profits from selling investments at a higher price than you paid

Passive Income Passive income refers to earnings that require little to no active effort once the initial setup is complete. This type of income is attractive because it allows you to continue making money even when you're not actively working. Passive income streams can take time to build, but once established, they can provide consistent revenue with minimal day-to-day involvement.

Examples of passive income include:

- Rental income from real estate properties
- Royalties from books, music, or patents
- Income from a blog, YouTube channel, or podcast that generates ad revenue or sponsorships
- Income from affiliate marketing or online courses

4. Entrepreneurial Income Starting a **side business** or **small business** is another way to diversify your income. Whether you're offering a product, service, or both, entrepreneurship allows you to be in control of your income and expand your earning potential. However, entrepreneurship typically requires more time and effort upfront before it can generate passive income.

Examples of entrepreneurial income include:

- Opening an online store
- Running a consulting business
- Creating digital products, like e-books or courses
- Providing a specialized service, like personal training or tutoring

How to Get Started with Diversifying Your Income

Now that you understand the concept of income diversification and the types of income streams available, it's time to take action. Here are a few steps to get started:

1. **Assess Your Skills and Interests** Start by evaluating your strengths and what you enjoy doing. Your **skills** and **hobbies** can often translate into profitable side hustles or entrepreneurial ventures. For example, if you're good at writing, consider freelance writing or blogging. If you're skilled at graphic design, consider creating digital products or offering design services.

2. **Start Small** You don't need to take on several income streams all at once. Start with one small project or investment and gradually scale it up as you become more comfortable. It's better to start small and grow organically than to overwhelm yourself with too many things at once.

3. **Invest in Learning** Educate yourself about the different types of income streams. Take courses, read books, or find mentors who can guide you. For example, if you're interested in investing, learning about the stock market or real estate can help you make informed decisions. The more knowledge you have, the better prepared you'll be to make wise financial choices.

4. **Create a Plan** Create a financial plan that includes your goals for diversifying your income. Whether it's generating an additional $500 per month from a side hustle or earning $1,000 from investments, setting clear and achievable goals will keep you motivated and focused on your long-term success.

Building a More Secure Financial Future

Understanding the concept of diversifying income is an essential step toward achieving financial security and independence. By spreading your income across different streams, you're not only reducing financial risks but also creating opportunities for wealth building and personal freedom. Diversification helps you weather life's uncertainties and allows you to enjoy the rewards of your hard work.

Building a Stronger Financial Future Through Income Diversification

Diversifying your income is not just a strategy—it's a mindset shift that empowers you to take control of your financial future. By building multiple streams of income, you protect yourself from the uncertainties of relying on a single paycheck or investment, and you open the door to greater financial opportunities and freedom. It's about creating a more secure, flexible, and rewarding life, where you're not bound by the limitations of one income source.

The beauty of diversifying your income lies in its ability to **complement your lifestyle**. It doesn't require drastic changes or sacrifices; instead, it's about finding opportunities that work for you, whether through a side hustle, investments, or creating passive income streams. Over time, as you add more sources of income, you'll notice a profound shift in your financial stability, your ability to achieve your goals faster, and your confidence in handling whatever life throws at you.

Start small, stay consistent, and remember that every step you take toward diversifying your income is a step closer to financial security and independence. You have the power to shape your financial future—by embracing the concept of multiple income streams, you're laying the foundation for a richer, more resilient life.

Chapter 14

Starting Your New Financial Journey: The First Step Toward Success

"An investment in knowledge pays the best interest." – Benjamin Franklin

Let's take a moment to look back at everything you've learned so far. You're now equipped with the knowledge to make smarter decisions with your money, and that's something to be proud of. So, let's break it down and see how these key lessons can really make a difference for you.

First, we dove into **budgeting**—and I'm sure by now, you've realized that a budget isn't just about restricting yourself. It's about **taking control**. It's about knowing exactly where your money is going so you can make sure it's being spent on things that matter most to you, like your savings, paying off debt, or treating yourself every once in a while. You're not just tracking your spending, you're making sure every dollar works for you, not the other way around.

Then, we talked about **saving**. I get it—putting money aside can feel like a challenge, especially when there's always something more pressing. But building your **emergency fund**? That's a game-changer. It's your safety net for those "just in case" moments—like when your car breaks down or you face an unexpected medical bill. It may seem like small steps at first, but over time, it adds up and gives you the confidence to handle whatever life throws your way without stressing about money.

We also tackled **credit**. You've probably heard how important it is, but now you understand why. Managing credit isn't just about using it wisely—it's about making sure it works for you. A good credit score can unlock better deals on loans, help you rent an apartment, or even land a job. Learning how to manage your credit responsibly means you're building a strong financial foundation for the future, one that keeps you out of debt and on track to meet your goals.

And then there's **investing**. I know it can sound intimidating, but you've learned that it's not as complex as it seems. Investing is just about making your money work for you. It's about putting your money into things like stocks or retirement funds that can grow over time. You've got the basics now, and the earlier you start—even if it's just a small amount—the more your money will grow. Imagine the power of **compound interest**: you start small, but over time, it adds up in a way that surprises you.

Finally, we discussed the importance of **diversifying your income**. Relying on just one paycheck? That's risky. Now you know that creating **multiple income streams**—like a side hustle or investing—gives you more security and freedom. It's all about making sure that, no matter what happens, you've got options. And that's a powerful feeling.

What you've learned here isn't just about checking off financial to-dos—it's about taking control of your financial life. It's about empowering you to make smarter choices, feel more confident, and build a solid future for yourself. Whether it's setting up a budget, saving for those "just in case" moments, improving your credit, making your money grow, or finding ways to earn extra cash, you now have the tools to start taking action. You don't have to wait for the perfect moment. The time is now, and you're ready to take the next step on your financial journey.

Building Confidence and Taking Control of Your Financial Future

You've taken an important step by reading this book and gaining the knowledge to take control of your finances—and that's something to be proud of. But here's the best part: **you are in charge of your financial future**. No matter where you're starting from or what your past financial habits might have been, you now have the tools to make a real change. And change, though challenging, is totally possible.

It's easy to feel overwhelmed by the idea of mastering money—there's so much to learn, and it can sometimes feel like you're facing an uphill battle. But I want you to know that **every step you take is progress**. Whether it's setting a budget, building your savings, or learning about credit, each small decision you make is moving you closer to financial freedom. **You are capable** of doing this. Financial success isn't reserved for a select few—it's available to anyone who is willing to learn, make better choices, and stay consistent.

You might encounter setbacks along the way, and that's okay. **Nobody's financial journey is perfect.** There will be moments where things don't go as planned—maybe you overspend one month or have a setback with debt. But remember, this is a process, not a race. The important thing is to keep going. It's the persistence to try again, the commitment to making small improvements, and the willingness to keep learning that will ultimately set you apart.

Whenever you face a challenge, remind yourself: financial growth is a journey. There will be ups and downs, but each step you take brings you closer to your goals. You're building habits that will serve you for a lifetime. And with each step, you're not just improving your finances—you're improving yourself, your mindset, and your ability to make decisions that align with the life you want to create.

Take a moment and acknowledge how far you've come. You've already made the first move toward a brighter, more secure future. Now, with the knowledge you've gained, you can make better decisions, build a foundation of savings and security, and ultimately create the life you've always wanted.

So, I want to leave you with this: You've got this. The road ahead may not always be easy, but with the right tools and a positive mindset, there's no limit to what you can achieve. Now is the time to start putting your plans into action. Your financial future is in your hands, and it's looking bright.

The Power of Small Steps and Consistency

You don't need to make huge changes all at once to see big results in your finances. In fact, **small, consistent actions** are often the most powerful way to build lasting financial success. It's easy to get caught up in the idea that you need to completely overhaul your financial situation overnight, but the truth is, small steps add up over time.

Think of it this way: if you save just a small portion of your income each month—maybe $20, $50, or even $100—that doesn't seem like much at first, right? But over a year, that small amount can turn into hundreds or even thousands of dollars. What's even more powerful is when you start investing, building an emergency fund, or paying down debt—those small actions compound over time. The key is to keep showing up and doing the work, no matter how small the task might seem.

Consistency is where the real magic happens. It's not about doing everything perfectly right away, it's about sticking with it, even when it feels difficult or when progress seems slow. By committing to making small improvements every day, week, or month, you start to build a financial routine that will work for you in the long run.

For example, if you start by budgeting every month, tracking your expenses, or even saving a small amount for an emergency fund, it may not feel like much at first. But over time, you'll start to see the benefits—whether it's having more money in your savings, paying off that nagging credit card debt, or feeling more confident in your financial decisions.

You might face moments of doubt, and that's normal. But trust in the power of small steps. Every time you make a conscious decision to save instead of spend, to pay down a little more debt, or to learn something new about money, you're creating momentum that will lead to big changes down the road. It's not about achieving perfection, but about creating habits that support the future you want.

In the end, consistency is what makes the difference between a fleeting effort and lasting success. Stick with it, stay focused, and remember that every little bit counts. You don't need to do everything all at once—just take one small step at a time, and those small steps will get you closer to the financial freedom you deserve.

Continuing Your Journey Toward Financial Success

Financial freedom isn't something that happens overnight—it's a journey that evolves over time. Just like any long-term goal, the path to financial security and independence is a continual process of learning, adjusting, and growing. The great thing about this journey is that it's yours to shape, and as you continue, you'll keep learning and making smarter decisions. There's no finish line, just milestones that you'll reach along the way.

One of the most important things to understand is that your financial journey will not be linear. You'll experience progress, but there will also be challenges and setbacks. And that's okay. What matters is how you adapt and how you keep moving forward, even when things don't go as planned. Life changes, and so will your financial priorities. You might face new obstacles—like a change in income, a medical emergency, or an unexpected expense—but you'll learn to navigate them with the tools and mindset you've built.

As your life changes, your financial goals will likely shift, too. Maybe you'll focus more on saving for a house as you get closer to buying one, or you might shift your focus to retirement savings as you start thinking about your future. Or perhaps you'll want to pursue new income streams or explore investing more as your financial situation improves. No matter where you are in your journey, there's always room to adjust, learn, and grow.

Think of your financial education as something that never really ends. There's always more to learn, more ways to improve, and new strategies to explore. Whether it's learning about new investment opportunities, fine-tuning your budget, or learning how to deal with taxes, there will always be new lessons and ways to improve. The key is to stay curious, keep learning, and adapt as you go.

Embrace the idea that financial growth is a lifelong commitment, and that's actually what makes it exciting. With each step you take, you're building a better foundation for the future. Your financial education doesn't stop here. Whether it's gaining new skills, refining what you know, or overcoming new challenges, the journey will continue to unfold—and with it, new opportunities and growth.

Remember, this isn't about perfection—it's about progress. The goal is to keep moving forward, adjusting when needed, and celebrating your wins along the way. As long as you stay committed, continue learning, and adapt to whatever comes next, you'll be building a brighter, more secure financial future for yourself. The journey is ongoing—and you're on the right track.

Setting the Stage for Financial Goals

Now that you've built a solid foundation of financial knowledge, it's time to set the stage for your financial goals. Goals give you direction, motivation, and a clear path to follow. Without them, it's easy to feel lost or uncertain about what steps to take next. Whether you want to pay off debt, save for a big purchase, or build wealth for the future, **setting clear, actionable goals is the key to making your financial dreams a reality**.

The first step in setting goals is to think about what you truly want to achieve. What's your vision for the future? Do you dream of owning a home, starting a business, traveling more, or securing a comfortable retirement? **Identify your "why"**—the reasons behind your financial goals. Understanding your motivations will keep you focused and help you stay on track, especially when challenges arise.

Once you've defined your goals, it's important to make them **specific** and **achievable**. Instead of saying, "I want to save money," try something like, "I want to save $1,000 for an emergency fund within the next 6 months." This gives you a clear target and a timeframe to work within, making the goal feel more manageable. Break your larger goals into smaller, more manageable milestones. For example, if you want to save $1,000 in six months, you'll need to save about $170 a month. Having smaller, specific targets makes it easier to track your progress and adjust if needed.

SMART goals are a great way to set yourself up for success. This stands for:

- **S**pecific
- **M**easurable
- **A**chievable
- **R**elevant
- **T**ime-bound

This method ensures your goals are clear and actionable. For instance, if your goal is to pay off credit card debt, you can make it SMART by saying, "I will pay off $500 of my credit card debt in the next 2 months by cutting back on unnecessary spending and putting any extra income toward my debt." This gives you a clear, measurable goal with a deadline, and a practical plan for achieving it.

Track your progress regularly to stay motivated and make adjustments as needed. If you find that you're falling short of a goal, don't be discouraged—adjusting the timeline or breaking the goal into smaller steps can help you get back on track without feeling overwhelmed. Remember, financial goals aren't about perfection—they're about moving forward, no matter the pace.

Lastly, **celebrate your wins**. Whether it's paying off a small debt, saving your first $500, or reaching a milestone in your investment journey, take time to recognize the progress you've made. Each step forward is a step closer to the financial freedom you're working toward.

Setting financial goals is the first step toward creating the future you want. You have the power to shape your financial journey—starting today. So, take a moment to think about your goals, write them down, and begin taking action. Your financial future is waiting.

Reinforcing the Importance of a Positive Money Mindset

As you continue on your financial journey, one of the most powerful tools you can have isn't found in a book, an app, or a spreadsheet. It's your money mindset—the way you think about and relate to money. Having a **positive money mindset** can be the difference between staying stuck in old habits and truly transforming your financial future.

Your beliefs about money are often shaped by your upbringing, experiences, and the environment you grew up in. If you've been taught to fear money, avoid discussing it, or feel like it's always out of reach, those beliefs can hold you back. But the good news is that **you have the power to change them**. Shifting your mindset about money can help you make better decisions, stay motivated, and unlock new opportunities.

Start by recognizing and challenging any negative or limiting beliefs you have about money. These beliefs might sound like: *"I'll never be able to save enough,"* or *"Money is for other people, not me."* These thoughts can hold you back, but the first step to overcoming them is simply being aware of them. Ask yourself where these beliefs come from, and if they're truly helping you move forward.

Once you've identified those limiting beliefs, it's time to replace them with empowering thoughts. Instead of focusing on scarcity, try shifting to a mindset of **abundance**. Believe that there is plenty of money in the world, and that you have the ability to earn, save, and invest. Instead of saying, *"I'll never get out of debt,"* try telling yourself, *"I'm taking steps every day to pay off my debt and create a better financial future."* Positive affirmations like this can slowly rewire your thinking and help you make decisions that align with your goals.

A positive money mindset isn't just about thinking happy thoughts—it's about taking **action with confidence**. When you believe that you can achieve financial goals, you're more likely to take the steps needed to make them happen. Whether it's creating a budget, starting a savings plan, or investing for the future, your belief in your ability to succeed will help you stay committed.

Also, remember that **money is a tool**, not something to fear or idolize.

When you approach money with a healthy mindset, it becomes something you can control and use to improve your life, rather than something that controls you. Money can give you the freedom to make choices, help others, and achieve your dreams. It's not about how much you have—it's about how you use it and the positive impact it can have on your life and the lives of those around you.

Lastly, **be patient with yourself**. Shifting your mindset takes time, especially if you've been holding onto old beliefs for a long time. But by practicing a positive money mindset and staying committed to your goals, you'll start to see the changes in your thoughts, your behavior, and your financial situation.

Fueling Your Drive to Take Action and Succeed

Remember, you are capable of financial success, and the journey starts with believing that you can get there. A positive mindset, combined with the knowledge and tools you've gained, will propel you toward the future you desire. So, as you continue on your path, keep nurturing that belief in yourself and your ability to make smart financial choices. Your mindset can truly be your greatest asset on the road to financial freedom.

You've come a long way on this journey, and now it's time to take that next step with confidence. The road to financial freedom is rarely a straight path, but every choice you make to improve your finances is a victory, no matter how small it may seem. What you've learned is just the beginning—now it's time to put that knowledge into action and start building the life you've always dreamed of.

Remember, you are in control. The power to transform your financial future is in your hands. **Every decision you make today shapes the life you'll have tomorrow.** You might feel like there's a lot to juggle, but by staying committed to the small steps you've already started, you'll build momentum that will carry you forward. Whether it's setting up a budget, saving for the future, or paying down debt, every step counts.

There will be challenges along the way. Setbacks happen, and they don't mean you've failed—they mean you're learning and growing. Financial success isn't about never making mistakes; it's about bouncing back stronger each time. The key is persistence. Keep your eyes on the bigger picture, and don't let temporary setbacks derail you from your goals.

You've got the knowledge now, and with the right mindset, you can achieve anything you set your mind to. You don't have to wait for the perfect moment. Start now, even if it's just with one small action—whether that's opening a savings account, setting up a budget, or taking the first steps toward investing. Every little bit moves you closer to your goal.

You are capable. You have everything you need to succeed. The journey ahead may take time, but with each step, you're getting closer to financial freedom. Your future doesn't depend on luck or a one-time big break—it depends on the decisions you make today and tomorrow. You've already taken the hardest step: committing to a better future.

Now, take a deep breath, gather your courage, and get started. The financial freedom you want is within your reach. All it takes is believing in yourself, taking action, and staying committed. You've got this. The best is yet to come.

Your Next Steps Toward Financial Freedom

As you wrap up this book, I want to take a moment to acknowledge how far you've come. You've taken the first step toward financial freedom by learning how to manage your money and make smart decisions. That's an accomplishment in itself, and it's something to be proud of. The road ahead may seem long, but with the knowledge, tools, and mindset you've gained, you're more than prepared to take on whatever comes next.

The most important thing to remember is that **this is just the beginning**. You don't need to have everything figured out right away. What matters is that you've started, and every decision you make from here will build the foundation for the future you want. You now have the power to take control of your finances, whether that's budgeting, saving, paying down debt, or investing in your future.

Keep in mind that the journey toward financial freedom is ongoing—there will be new things to learn, new goals to set, and new challenges to overcome. But with each step, you'll get closer to creating the life you've always dreamed of. Your financial future is in your hands, and it's brighter than ever before.

I want to leave you with this: **You are capable of achieving everything you want.** No matter where you started or what obstacles you face, you have the knowledge, the mindset, and the determination to make your financial goals a reality. So, don't wait for the perfect time—start today. Each small step you take will bring you closer to the financial freedom and security you deserve.

Thank you for taking this journey with me. Here's to your financial success and the incredible future ahead. You've got this!

Printed in Great Britain
by Amazon

59867784R00092